Mobile Security Fundamentals

How to Protect Your Smartphone, Personal Data, and Online Accounts From Modern Cyber Threats

By Joe Correa

Published by Live Stronger Faster

This book is for educational and informational purposes only. The author and publisher are not engaged in rendering legal, financial, or other professional advice. Readers should consult a qualified professional before making any financial decisions.

First Edition

Table of Contents

Introduction

Welcome to *Mobile Security Fundamentals: How to Protect Your Smartphone, Personal Data, and Online Accounts From Modern Cyber Threats*. Whether you use an Android device, an iPhone, a tablet, or multiple connected mobile devices, you are carrying one of the most powerful pieces of technology ever created. Your smartphone serves as your communication center, personal assistant, digital wallet, entertainment system, workplace, navigation tool, banking terminal, camera, and gateway to nearly every aspect of your daily life. It contains personal conversations, financial information, family photos, business documents, passwords, medical information, and countless details about your habits, interests, and activities. In many ways, your smartphone knows more about you than almost any other possession you own.

Unfortunately, the same technology that makes smartphones so useful also makes them attractive targets for cybercriminals. Every year, millions of people become victims of identity theft, account takeovers, mobile malware infections, financial fraud, phishing attacks, and privacy violations. Many users believe that cyberattacks only happen to large corporations, wealthy individuals, or government agencies. The reality is that cybercriminals often target ordinary people because they tend to have fewer security protections and are less likely to recognize warning signs. Every smartphone user is a potential target.

One of the biggest misconceptions about cybersecurity is the belief that mobile devices are automatically safe. Many people assume that because they purchased a modern smartphone from a trusted manufacturer, security is guaranteed. While modern devices include impressive security features, they are only one layer of protection. Human behavior remains the weakest link in most security incidents. A sophisticated smartphone can still be compromised if its owner clicks a malicious link, installs an unsafe application, reuses weak passwords, or connects to an insecure network. Technology can help protect us, but understanding how threats work is equally important.

The mobile threat landscape has evolved dramatically over the last decade. Early mobile phones offered limited functionality and contained relatively little personal information. Today's smartphones function as portable computers connected to vast digital ecosystems. Cybercriminals have adapted accordingly. Attackers now develop malware specifically designed for mobile devices. Fraudsters create convincing text message scams that imitate banks, delivery companies, and government agencies. Hackers search for weaknesses in applications, wireless networks, and online accounts. Criminal organizations operate sophisticated schemes designed to steal personal information and financial assets from unsuspecting users around the world.

Many of these attacks are surprisingly simple. A single text message claiming that a package delivery has failed may persuade a user to click a malicious link. A fake login page can capture usernames and passwords. A fraudulent application may secretly collect personal information or monitor device activity. An unsecured public Wi-Fi network can expose sensitive communications. These attacks succeed not because the technology is complex, but because they exploit human trust, curiosity, urgency, and convenience.

The good news is that effective mobile security does not require advanced technical expertise. You do not need to become a cybersecurity engineer, software developer, or digital forensics expert to significantly improve your protection. Most successful security practices are based on awareness, habits, and simple defensive measures. Understanding how attackers operate allows you to recognize risks before they become problems. Small changes in behavior can dramatically reduce your exposure to cyber threats.

This book was created to provide a practical foundation in mobile security. Rather than overwhelming you with technical jargon, complex programming concepts, or advanced cybersecurity theory, this guide focuses on real-world protection strategies that anyone can implement. You will learn how to identify common threats, strengthen your device security, safeguard your accounts, protect your personal information, and develop habits that reduce risk. The goal is not to create fear but to build confidence. When you understand how mobile threats work, you gain the ability to use technology safely and responsibly.

Throughout this book, you will discover that cybersecurity is not a one-time task but an ongoing process. New threats emerge regularly, and attackers continuously adapt their methods. Security requires awareness, maintenance, and continuous learning. Fortunately, the fundamental principles of protection remain consistent. Strong authentication, secure software practices, cautious online behavior, and proactive monitoring form the foundation of effective security regardless of how technology evolves.

Another important concept you will encounter is the balance between convenience and security. Modern technology often prioritizes speed and ease of use. Features such as automatic logins, saved passwords, cloud synchronization, and location tracking provide convenience but can also introduce risks when not properly managed. Effective cybersecurity does not mean eliminating convenience entirely. Instead, it means making informed decisions about which features to use, how to configure them securely, and when additional safeguards are necessary.

Privacy is another major theme throughout this book. While security focuses on protecting systems and information from unauthorized access, privacy concerns how information is collected, shared, stored, and used. Many mobile applications gather significant amounts of personal data, including location information, contact lists, browsing habits, device identifiers, and behavioral patterns. Understanding what information is collected and how to control it is essential for protecting your digital identity in today's interconnected world.

You may be surprised to learn how much information your smartphone generates every day. Mobile devices continuously interact with cellular networks, Wi-Fi access points, Bluetooth devices, GPS satellites, cloud services, applications, and websites. Each interaction creates data that may reveal valuable information about your activities and preferences. While much of this data collection supports legitimate services and features, users should understand how their information is being handled and what steps they can take to maintain greater control.

Cybersecurity is not solely about protecting technology; it is about protecting people. Behind every account, password, photograph, financial transaction, and personal message is a human being whose life can be affected by a security incident. Identity theft can damage financial stability. Data breaches can expose sensitive information. Account takeovers can disrupt personal and professional relationships. By improving your cybersecurity knowledge, you are protecting not only your devices but also your reputation, finances, relationships, and peace of mind.

As you progress through this book, you will begin to view your smartphone differently. Rather than seeing it simply as a communication device, you will recognize it as an important digital asset that deserves protection. You will learn to identify suspicious behavior, evaluate risks more effectively, and make smarter decisions regarding apps, networks, accounts, and online interactions. These skills are valuable not only for your own security but also for helping family members, friends, and colleagues stay safe.

The principles introduced in this book also serve as the foundation for the remaining books in the *Mobile Security & App Protection Academy* series. Future volumes will explore application privacy, Android security, iPhone protection, mobile banking security, social media safety, encrypted communications, family protection strategies, and advanced cybersecurity defenses. Together, these books will provide a comprehensive roadmap for securing every aspect of your mobile digital life.

Technology will continue to evolve, and cyber threats will continue to adapt. However, one truth remains constant: knowledge is one of the most powerful security tools available. Every lesson you learn, every secure habit you develop, and every informed decision you make strengthens your defenses against digital threats. Cybersecurity is not about achieving perfect protection; it is about reducing risk, improving awareness, and making it more difficult for attackers to succeed.

Thank you for beginning this journey into mobile security. By investing your time in learning these essential skills, you are taking an important step toward protecting your information, preserving your privacy, and securing your digital future. The threats may be real, but so are the solutions. With the right knowledge and consistent habits, you can enjoy the benefits of modern technology while significantly reducing your exposure to cyber risks. Let us begin by exploring the foundations of mobile security and the practical steps every smartphone user should understand.

Chapter 1

Understanding the Modern Mobile Threat Landscape

Your smartphone is one of the most important devices you own. It stores personal information, financial data, private conversations, photos, videos, contacts, passwords, work documents, and access to countless online services. In many cases, a smartphone provides access to nearly every aspect of a person's digital life. Because of this, mobile devices have become valuable targets for cybercriminals. Understanding the mobile threat landscape is the first step toward protecting yourself from modern cyber risks.

The mobile threat landscape refers to the collection of dangers, vulnerabilities, attack methods, and security challenges that affect smartphones and mobile devices. Unlike traditional desktop computers, mobile devices are constantly connected to networks and travel everywhere with their users. They connect to public Wi-Fi networks, Bluetooth devices, cellular networks, cloud services, and mobile applications throughout the day. Each connection creates opportunities for both convenience and potential security risks.

One of the most common threats facing smartphone users today is phishing. Phishing attacks attempt to trick users into revealing sensitive information such as usernames, passwords, credit card numbers, or personal details. While phishing originally focused on email, modern attackers frequently use text messages, social media messages, and messaging applications. This mobile-focused phishing is often referred to as "smishing," which combines SMS and phishing. A text message may claim that a package delivery failed, a bank account requires verification, or a payment is overdue. The message often creates a sense of urgency to encourage immediate action without careful thought.

Cybercriminals understand human psychology remarkably well. They know that fear, curiosity, excitement, and urgency often cause people to make poor security decisions. A message warning that an account will be suspended may encourage immediate action. A notification claiming that someone has accessed a bank account may create panic. A promise of free money, prizes, or discounts may trigger excitement. These emotional responses are often more effective than technical attacks because they target human behavior rather than software vulnerabilities.

Another major threat involves malicious applications. Mobile applications provide useful functionality, but not every app available online is trustworthy. Some applications are designed specifically to steal information, monitor activity, display intrusive advertising, or install additional malware. Attackers may create applications that appear legitimate while secretly collecting sensitive data in the background. Users who download apps from unofficial sources face particularly high risks because these applications may not undergo security screening.

Mobile malware continues to evolve rapidly. Malware is software designed to perform harmful actions without the user's knowledge or consent. Some malware steals passwords and account credentials. Other malware records keystrokes, monitors communications, or captures screenshots. Certain forms of malware can even gain administrative control over a device. Although mobile operating systems include security protections, attackers continuously search for new ways to bypass those defenses.

Ransomware has also expanded into the mobile environment. Traditional ransomware encrypts files and demands payment for their release. Mobile ransomware may lock devices, block access to data, or display fraudulent warnings claiming legal violations. Victims are instructed to pay money to restore access. Unfortunately, payment does not always guarantee recovery. The best defense against ransomware is prevention through secure habits and regular backups.

Public Wi-Fi networks present another significant risk. Airports, hotels, restaurants, shopping centers, and coffee shops often provide free internet access. While convenient, these networks may expose users to various threats. Attackers sometimes create fake Wi-Fi networks that imitate legitimate services. Unsuspecting users connect to these networks and unknowingly allow attackers to intercept data. Even legitimate public networks may lack sufficient security protections.

Bluetooth technology introduces additional security considerations. Bluetooth enables wireless communication between devices such as headphones, smartwatches, speakers, and vehicles. While generally secure when properly configured, Bluetooth can create vulnerabilities if left enabled unnecessarily. Attackers may exploit Bluetooth weaknesses to access devices, track users, or transfer malicious files. Limiting Bluetooth use to trusted devices reduces unnecessary exposure.

Account compromise remains one of the most damaging forms of cybercrime. Many users reuse passwords across multiple accounts. When one account is compromised through a data breach, attackers often test the same credentials on banking, social media, email, and shopping platforms. This technique, known as credential stuffing, allows criminals to gain access to multiple services using a single stolen password. Strong password management practices significantly reduce this risk.

Identity theft continues to affect millions of people each year. Cybercriminals collect personal information from various sources and use it to impersonate victims. Stolen information may include names, addresses, phone numbers, social security numbers, banking information, and account credentials. Mobile devices often contain many of these details, making smartphone security an important component of identity protection.

Mobile users must also be aware of privacy threats. Not every threat involves direct financial theft. Some organizations collect extensive information about user behavior, locations, interests, and activities. Applications may track movements, monitor browsing habits, or gather personal preferences. While some data collection supports legitimate services, excessive tracking can create privacy concerns. Understanding app permissions and privacy settings helps users maintain greater control over their information.

Software vulnerabilities represent another major security concern. Vulnerabilities are weaknesses within software that attackers can exploit. Mobile operating system developers regularly release security updates to address newly discovered vulnerabilities. Users who delay updates may leave their devices exposed to known security flaws. Keeping operating systems and applications current is one of the simplest yet most effective security measures available.

Social engineering attacks deserve special attention because they target human behavior rather than technology. Social engineering involves manipulating individuals into performing actions that compromise security. Attackers may impersonate technical support representatives, financial institutions, employers, or government agencies. The goal is often to gain trust and obtain information voluntarily. Understanding common social engineering techniques makes it easier to recognize suspicious interactions before damage occurs.

As mobile technology continues to evolve, new threats will inevitably emerge. Artificial intelligence, connected devices, digital payments, cloud services, and advanced mobile applications create exciting opportunities while also introducing new security challenges. Cybersecurity is therefore not a destination but an ongoing process of awareness, education, and adaptation. Individuals who remain informed and proactive are far better equipped to protect themselves against evolving threats.

The most important lesson from this chapter is that cybersecurity begins with awareness. Many attacks succeed because users are unaware of risks or underestimate their vulnerability. By understanding the modern mobile threat landscape, you establish the foundation needed to recognize dangers, make informed decisions, and build strong security habits. Knowledge transforms cybersecurity from a confusing technical topic into a practical life skill that benefits every smartphone user.

David received a text message

David considered himself reasonably careful with technology. He owned a modern smartphone, used popular apps, and believed that major cyberattacks happened to corporations rather than ordinary individuals. Like millions of people, he assumed that his device's built-in security features would protect him from most problems. He rarely thought about cybersecurity and focused instead on convenience.

One Monday morning, David received a text message claiming that a package delivery had failed. The message included a link and instructed him to update his delivery information. Since he had recently ordered several items online, the message seemed believable. Without much hesitation, he clicked the link and entered his personal information into what appeared to be a legitimate website.

Several days later, David noticed unusual activity on one of his online accounts. Password reset notifications appeared unexpectedly. A social media account became inaccessible. Then unauthorized purchases appeared on a credit card statement. What initially seemed like a minor inconvenience quickly evolved into a serious problem.

As David attempted to understand what happened, he discovered that the delivery notification had been a phishing attack. The website he visited was designed specifically to capture personal information. Once attackers obtained his credentials, they used them to access additional accounts because he had reused similar passwords across multiple services.

Frustrated and overwhelmed, David contacted financial institutions, changed passwords, reported fraud, and spent countless hours recovering access to accounts. The process was stressful, time-consuming, and emotionally draining. He began realizing how interconnected his digital life had become. A compromise affecting one account created problems across many others.

Determined to avoid future incidents, David started learning about mobile security. He researched phishing attacks, malware, password management, and privacy protection. The more he learned, the more he realized how many threats existed that he had never previously considered. He discovered that cybersecurity was not reserved for experts; it involved practical habits anyone could learn.

One lesson particularly surprised him. Most successful cyberattacks did not rely on sophisticated hacking techniques. Instead, they exploited predictable human behavior. Attackers created urgency, fear, curiosity, or excitement to encourage poor decisions. Understanding this principle fundamentally changed how David approached digital interactions.

Over the following months, David implemented numerous improvements. He enabled multifactor authentication on important accounts. He installed software updates promptly. He stopped reusing passwords and adopted a password manager. He reviewed application permissions and removed unnecessary apps. He became cautious about unexpected messages and links.

One afternoon, he received another suspicious text message claiming that his bank account had been compromised. Unlike before, he recognized several warning signs immediately. The message created urgency, requested personal information, and included an unfamiliar link. Instead of responding, he contacted his bank directly through official channels. The bank confirmed that the message was fraudulent.

That experience reinforced the value of cybersecurity awareness. David realized that knowledge had transformed him from an easy target into a much more difficult victim. The attackers had not changed their methods; his awareness had changed his response. What previously would have triggered panic now triggered caution and verification.

As David shared his experiences with friends and family, he discovered that many people had encountered similar situations. Some had experienced fraudulent calls. Others had clicked suspicious links or installed questionable applications. Many assumed cybersecurity was too technical for them to understand. David explained that the most important defenses involved awareness, critical thinking, and consistent habits rather than advanced technical expertise.

Years later, David still encountered occasional scams and suspicious messages. Cyber threats had not disappeared. However, he approached them with confidence rather than fear. He understood the tactics attackers used and recognized warning signs early. More importantly, he viewed cybersecurity as an ongoing practice rather than a one-time task.

The incident that initially seemed like a disaster ultimately became a valuable lesson. It taught David that smartphones contain far more than contacts and photos. They contain pieces of our identities, finances, relationships, and daily lives. Protecting them requires knowledge, vigilance, and responsibility.

As he continued strengthening his security habits, David often reflected on how a simple phishing message had changed his perspective forever. The experience revealed a truth that applies to every smartphone user: cybersecurity begins with awareness. Once individuals understand the threats around them, they gain the power to make smarter decisions and protect themselves in an increasingly connected world.

The modern mobile threat landscape will continue evolving. New technologies will emerge, attackers will develop new techniques, and digital life will become even more interconnected. Yet the lessons David learned remain timeless. Awareness, caution, education, and proactive security habits form the foundation of effective protection. Those who embrace these principles are far better prepared to navigate the digital world safely and confidently.

Chapter 2

How Smartphones Store, Share, and Protect Your Information

One of the most important steps in becoming more secure is understanding exactly how your smartphone handles information. Most users interact with their devices every day without fully understanding what happens behind the scenes when they send a message, take a photo, download an application, browse a website, make a payment, or log in to an account. While modern smartphones make these activities appear simple and seamless, an enormous amount of data is constantly being collected, stored, processed, and transmitted. Understanding this process helps users make smarter security decisions and recognize where potential risks may exist.

A smartphone functions as a small but powerful computer. It contains hardware components such as processors, memory chips, storage drives, cameras, microphones, wireless communication systems, and sensors. Together, these components collect and manage information continuously. Every text message, email, photograph, video recording, voice memo, website visit, and application interaction generates data. Some of this information remains stored directly on the device, while other information may be transmitted to cloud services or external servers.

The concept of data storage is central to smartphone security. Storage refers to the location where information is saved. Modern smartphones store thousands of files and data records. Photos are saved in galleries. Contacts are stored in databases. Applications create files containing settings and user preferences. Browsers store cookies, browsing history, and cached content. Messaging applications maintain conversation histories. Financial apps may store transaction records and account information. The amount of information contained within a smartphone often surprises users once they begin examining it closely.

Many people assume that deleting information immediately removes it from a device. In reality, deletion often works differently. When a file is deleted, the operating system may simply mark the storage space as available for future use. Until new information replaces the old data, portions of the deleted content may remain recoverable. This is one reason why properly resetting and erasing devices before selling or recycling them is so important. Simply deleting files does not always eliminate them completely.

Cloud storage has transformed how smartphones manage information. Services such as photo backups, file synchronization, contact storage, and cloud-based messaging allow users to access information across multiple devices. While cloud services provide convenience and backup protection, they also introduce additional security considerations. Information stored in the cloud may be protected by strong encryption and security controls, but users must still secure their accounts properly. A weak password protecting a cloud account can expose years of personal data even if the smartphone itself remains secure.

Data transmission is another critical aspect of mobile security. Whenever a smartphone communicates with websites, applications, cloud services, or other devices, information travels across networks. These transmissions may occur through cellular networks, Wi-Fi connections, Bluetooth communications, or other wireless technologies. Modern security protocols help protect this information through encryption, which converts readable information into coded data that can only be understood by authorized parties.

Encryption is one of the most powerful security tools available today. When data is encrypted, it becomes extremely difficult for unauthorized individuals to read or understand the information. Many modern smartphones automatically encrypt stored data. Secure websites use encrypted connections to protect login credentials and financial transactions. Messaging applications increasingly offer encrypted communication options. While encryption is not a perfect solution, it significantly increases the difficulty of intercepting or accessing sensitive information.

Passwords play a major role in protecting stored information. Every account associated with a smartphone serves as a gateway to personal data. Email accounts, cloud storage services, banking applications, social media platforms, and shopping websites often contain sensitive information. If attackers gain access to a single account, they may be able to access much more than initially expected. Strong, unique passwords remain one of the simplest and most effective security measures available.

Authentication refers to the process of verifying identity before granting access. Traditional passwords represent one form of authentication. Modern smartphones also support biometric authentication methods such as fingerprint recognition and facial recognition. These technologies provide convenience while adding additional security layers. However, users should understand that no authentication system is perfect. Combining multiple forms of authentication often provides stronger protection than relying on a single method.

Applications constantly collect and process information. Some applications require access to contacts, location data, cameras, microphones, or storage systems to function properly. Others request permissions that may exceed their legitimate needs. Users should carefully evaluate permission requests before granting access. A navigation application may reasonably require location information, while a simple flashlight application likely does not. Reviewing permissions regularly helps minimize unnecessary data exposure.

Location tracking deserves special attention because it reveals significant details about daily activities. Smartphones can determine location using GPS satellites, cellular towers, Wi-Fi networks, and Bluetooth signals. Many applications request location access to provide useful features. However, constant location tracking can reveal where users live, work, shop, travel, and spend time. Understanding location settings allows users to balance convenience with privacy.

Modern smartphones also collect behavioral information. This includes how applications are used, which websites are visited, how often services are accessed, and various usage patterns. Technology companies often use this information to improve services, personalize content, and deliver targeted advertising. While these activities may provide benefits, users should understand what information is being collected and how it is being used.

Operating systems such as Android and iOS include built-in security frameworks designed to protect users. These systems isolate applications from one another, manage permissions, monitor suspicious activity, and enforce security policies. Security updates regularly improve these protections by addressing newly discovered vulnerabilities. Installing updates promptly ensures that users benefit from the latest security improvements and threat protections.

Data backups provide another essential layer of protection. Smartphones may be lost, stolen, damaged, or infected by malware. Without backups, valuable information can be permanently lost. Regular backups ensure that important photos, contacts, documents, and settings remain recoverable. Effective security involves both preventing unauthorized access and ensuring information remains available when needed.

Users should also understand metadata. Metadata is information about information. For example, a photograph may contain details about when it was taken, where it was captured, what device created it, and other technical characteristics. Documents, emails, and messages often contain metadata as well. While metadata may seem harmless, it can reveal substantial information about user behavior and activities.

Many cyberattacks focus on obtaining information rather than damaging devices. Criminals value personal information because it can be sold, used for identity theft, leveraged for financial fraud, or exploited in future attacks. Understanding how information flows through smartphones helps users recognize why security measures are necessary. Every piece of personal information has potential value to an attacker.

Digital privacy and digital security are closely related but distinct concepts. Security focuses on preventing unauthorized access and protecting systems from threats. Privacy focuses on controlling how information is collected, used, shared, and stored. Both are important. A device can be highly secure while still collecting extensive personal information. Likewise, strong privacy controls may not prevent security breaches. Effective protection requires attention to both areas.

The more users understand how smartphones store, share, and protect information, the better equipped they become to make informed decisions. Security is no longer simply about preventing hackers from accessing devices. It involves understanding the entire ecosystem of data collection, storage, transmission, authentication, and privacy management. Knowledge empowers users to take control of their digital lives rather than relying solely on technology providers to protect them.

Ultimately, your smartphone serves as a digital extension of your life. The information it contains represents your memories, relationships, finances, activities, and identity. Understanding how that information is handled is one of the most valuable cybersecurity skills you can develop. Awareness creates stronger habits, smarter decisions, and better protection against modern digital threats.

Maria attended a cybersecurity seminar

Maria loved technology. Her smartphone helped her manage nearly every aspect of her life. She used it to communicate with family, coordinate work projects, manage finances, store photos, navigate unfamiliar locations, shop online, and stay connected through social media. Like many people, she rarely thought about what happened behind the scenes when she used her device.

One afternoon, Maria attended a cybersecurity seminar hosted by her employer. During the presentation, the instructor asked a simple question: "How much information does your smartphone know about you?" Maria assumed the answer was limited to contacts, photos, and messages. She soon discovered that the reality was far more extensive.

The instructor explained how smartphones continuously generate data. Location histories revealed travel patterns. Search histories reflected interests and concerns. Applications tracked usage habits. Photos contained hidden metadata. Cloud accounts stored years of personal information. Every digital activity created data points that collectively painted a detailed picture of a person's life.

Curious, Maria began exploring her own device after returning home. She reviewed account settings, application permissions, cloud backups, and privacy controls. She was surprised to discover that several applications had access to her location at all times. Some apps had permission to access contacts, photos, microphones, and cameras even though those permissions seemed unnecessary.

As she continued investigating, Maria discovered years of stored information within her cloud accounts. Thousands of photos, documents, emails, notes, and backups had accumulated over time. While she appreciated the convenience of having everything available, she also realized how valuable this information would be to anyone who gained unauthorized access.

Determined to improve her security, Maria began making changes. She reviewed every application installed on her phone. Apps she no longer used were removed. Permissions were adjusted to match legitimate needs. Location access was limited whenever possible. She enabled multifactor authentication on important accounts and strengthened weak passwords.

Several weeks later, Maria received an email notifying her that an online service she had used years earlier had experienced a data breach. User account information had been exposed, including email addresses and passwords. Because Maria had already strengthened her security practices, she felt prepared rather than panicked. She immediately changed credentials associated with that service and reviewed related accounts.

The incident reinforced the importance of understanding how information flows through digital systems. Maria realized that security was not just about protecting a physical device. It involved protecting a complex network of accounts, services, applications, and data repositories connected to that device.

Over time, Maria became more intentional about privacy as well. She reviewed what information applications collected and how companies used her data. She adjusted advertising preferences, disabled unnecessary tracking features, and became more selective about which services she trusted. While she understood that complete privacy was unrealistic in a connected world, she appreciated having greater control over her information.

One day, a friend named Alex complained about losing access to years of family photos after a smartphone malfunction. Alex had never configured backups and assumed the photos would always remain available. Unfortunately, most of the images could not be recovered. Watching Alex's frustration convinced Maria to double-check her own backup systems. She verified that important files were securely stored and recoverable if needed.

As months passed, Maria noticed something interesting. The more she understood about technology, the less intimidating cybersecurity seemed. What once felt complicated and overwhelming became manageable. Concepts such as encryption, authentication, permissions, and backups were no longer mysterious technical terms. They were practical tools that helped protect her digital life.

Eventually, Maria became the person friends and family consulted when they had security questions. She explained how smartphones store information, why strong passwords matter, how cloud services work, and why permissions should be reviewed regularly. Her goal was not to create fear but to help others understand the importance of awareness.

One evening, Maria looked through her smartphone and reflected on how much of her life it contained. Photographs documented years of memories. Messages preserved important conversations. Financial applications managed significant assets. Health apps tracked personal goals. The device represented far more than hardware and software. It served as a digital archive of her experiences, relationships, and identity.

That realization reinforced the lessons she had learned. Understanding how smartphones store, share, and protect information was not merely a technical skill. It was a life skill. The more informed she became, the more confidently she could navigate the digital world while protecting what mattered most.

As technology continued evolving, Maria knew new challenges would emerge. Yet she also understood that the fundamental principles remained the same. Awareness, education, responsible habits, and proactive security practices would continue providing a strong foundation for protection. By understanding how information moves through her digital ecosystem, she had gained one of the most valuable tools in cybersecurity: the ability to make informed decisions.

The knowledge she gained did not eliminate every risk, but it transformed her relationship with technology. Instead of blindly trusting systems she did not understand, she became an active participant in protecting her own digital future. That confidence, built on understanding and awareness, became one of her greatest cybersecurity assets.

Chapter 3

Essential Mobile Security Habits Every User Should Develop

The most powerful cybersecurity tool available is not a smartphone, antivirus application, firewall, or security program. It is human behavior. While technology provides important protections, the habits users develop often determine whether security measures succeed or fail. Many cyberattacks do not occur because technology is weak; they occur because users unknowingly make decisions that expose themselves to unnecessary risk. Developing strong mobile security habits creates a foundation that protects against a wide variety of threats and significantly reduces the likelihood of becoming a victim.

One of the most important habits every smartphone user should develop is maintaining a security-first mindset. This does not mean living in fear or assuming every interaction is dangerous. Instead, it means approaching digital activities with awareness and healthy skepticism. Just as people lock their homes, secure their vehicles, and protect valuable possessions, they should also protect their digital lives. A security-first mindset encourages users to think before clicking, verify before trusting, and evaluate risks before taking action.

Strong password management is among the most critical security habits. Many users continue to rely on simple passwords that are easy to remember but also easy for attackers to guess. Others reuse the same password across multiple accounts. These practices create significant vulnerabilities. If one account becomes compromised, attackers may gain access to many others. Every important account should have a unique password that combines length, complexity, and unpredictability. Password managers can help users generate and store strong credentials without requiring them to memorize dozens of different passwords.

Multifactor authentication adds another essential layer of protection. Even the strongest password can potentially be stolen through phishing attacks, malware, or data breaches. Multifactor authentication requires an additional verification step before access is granted. This may involve a temporary code, authentication application, hardware token, biometric verification, or another method. By requiring multiple forms of verification, multifactor authentication makes unauthorized access far more difficult.

Keeping devices updated is another habit that cannot be overstated. Software updates often include security patches that address vulnerabilities discovered by researchers and developers. Cybercriminals actively search for devices running outdated software because known weaknesses may be easier to exploit. Delaying updates leaves users exposed to threats that may already have effective solutions available. Enabling automatic updates whenever possible helps ensure devices remain protected against emerging risks.

Application management is another area where strong habits make a significant difference. Many users install applications without carefully reviewing what they do, who developed them, or what permissions they request. Before downloading an application, users should evaluate its legitimacy, read reviews, examine developer information, and verify that it comes from a trusted source. Applications should only request permissions necessary for their intended functionality. Unnecessary permissions can create privacy and security risks.

Regularly reviewing installed applications is equally important. Over time, smartphones often accumulate apps that are no longer used. Each installed application represents potential risk because vulnerabilities may exist within the software. Removing unnecessary applications reduces the attack surface available to cybercriminals. It also helps improve device performance and simplify privacy management.

Another critical habit involves carefully evaluating links, attachments, and messages. Cybercriminals frequently disguise malicious content as legitimate communications. A message may appear to come from a bank, shipping company, employer, friend, or government agency. Users should verify unexpected requests independently before responding. Suspicious messages should be approached cautiously, particularly if they create urgency, request personal information, or encourage immediate action.

Email security remains highly relevant in the mobile environment. Smartphones make it easy to quickly read and respond to messages, but convenience can sometimes reduce caution. Users should examine sender addresses carefully, verify unexpected attachments, and avoid clicking unfamiliar links. Taking a few extra moments to evaluate a message can prevent significant security incidents.

Public Wi-Fi usage requires special attention. Free wireless internet is convenient, but not all networks are trustworthy. Attackers may create fraudulent networks designed to intercept user traffic. Even legitimate public networks may expose users to unnecessary risks. Sensitive activities such as banking, financial transactions, and account management should generally be avoided on unsecured public networks. Virtual private networks, commonly known as VPNs, can provide additional protection when using public internet connections.

Bluetooth management is another frequently overlooked habit. While Bluetooth technology enables useful wireless connections, leaving it enabled continuously can increase exposure to potential threats. Users should disable Bluetooth when not actively using it and avoid pairing with unknown devices. Maintaining control over wireless connections reduces unnecessary security risks.

Device locking is a simple but highly effective habit. Smartphones should always be protected by strong screen locks. PINs, passwords, fingerprints, and facial recognition systems help prevent unauthorized access if a device is lost or stolen. A surprising number of users still rely on weak codes or disable locking features entirely. Physical access often provides attackers with opportunities to bypass other security controls, making device locking a fundamental defense.

Data backup practices are equally important. Even the most secure device can be lost, damaged, stolen, or affected by software failures. Regular backups ensure valuable information remains recoverable. Photos, contacts, documents, messages, and settings should be backed up using secure methods. Effective cybersecurity includes protecting both confidentiality and availability.

Privacy awareness is becoming increasingly important in today's digital environment. Users should understand what information applications collect, how that information is used, and who receives access to it. Privacy settings should be reviewed periodically. Limiting unnecessary data collection reduces exposure and gives users greater control over their digital identities.

Security awareness training is another valuable habit. Cybersecurity is not a skill learned once and then forgotten. Threats evolve continuously. New scams, vulnerabilities, and attack methods emerge regularly. Users who stay informed about current threats are better prepared to recognize and avoid them. Reading security news, following trusted cybersecurity resources, and learning about emerging risks can significantly improve protection.

Another important habit involves separating personal and professional activities whenever possible. Many users conduct work-related activities on personal devices and personal activities on work devices. While this arrangement is often necessary, maintaining clear boundaries reduces risk. Sensitive information should be handled carefully, and organizational security policies should be followed consistently.

Social media behavior also affects mobile security. Users often share more information than they realize. Public posts may reveal locations, routines, travel plans, family details, employment information, and other sensitive data. Cybercriminals frequently gather publicly available information to support social engineering attacks. Practicing thoughtful sharing habits helps reduce exposure.

Perhaps the most valuable habit of all is slowing down. Many successful cyberattacks rely on impulsive reactions. Attackers create urgency specifically to prevent careful evaluation. Taking a moment to pause, think, and verify information can prevent countless security incidents. Patience and awareness are often more effective than any software solution.

Building strong security habits requires consistency. Individual actions may seem small, but together they create a powerful defense system. Cybersecurity is not achieved through a single tool or action. It is the result of many good decisions repeated over time. The habits developed today can provide protection for years to come, helping users navigate the digital world with confidence and resilience.

A cybersecurity professional named Rachel

Michael considered himself a typical smartphone user. He enjoyed technology, used dozens of applications, managed his finances online, and stayed connected through social media. While he occasionally heard news reports about cyberattacks, he assumed they were problems that affected other people. He believed that because he was not wealthy or famous, cybercriminals would have little interest in targeting him.

One afternoon, Michael attended a technology workshop offered by his community center. A cybersecurity professional named Rachel delivered a presentation about mobile security habits. Rather than discussing complex technical concepts, she focused on everyday behaviors. Her message was simple: cybersecurity is often determined by habits rather than technology.

Michael found the idea interesting but somewhat difficult to believe. His smartphone contained advanced security features. Surely that was enough. Yet as Rachel shared real-world examples, he began to reconsider. She described individuals who lost money through phishing scams, had social media accounts hijacked, or became victims of identity theft because of small mistakes that could have been prevented.

Motivated by curiosity, Michael decided to evaluate his own habits. The results surprised him. He used the same password across multiple accounts. Several applications had not been updated for months. Bluetooth remained enabled constantly. He frequently connected to public Wi-Fi networks without considering security risks. He rarely reviewed application permissions and had never enabled multifactor authentication.

Instead of feeling overwhelmed, Michael chose to improve one habit at a time. He began by installing a password manager and replacing weak passwords with strong, unique alternatives. Although the process required effort, he quickly appreciated the added security. Next, he enabled multifactor authentication on email, banking, and social media accounts.

Over the following weeks, Michael continued making improvements. He removed unused applications, reviewed permissions, updated software regularly, and configured automatic backups. He also became more cautious about links and messages. Rather than reacting immediately to unexpected communications, he developed the habit of verifying requests independently.

One day, Michael received a text message claiming that his bank account required immediate verification. The message included a link and warned that access would be suspended if he failed to respond. Several months earlier, he likely would have clicked without hesitation. This time, however, he paused. Remembering Rachel's advice, he contacted his bank directly using the official phone number listed on his account.

The representative confirmed that no such notification had been sent. The message was a phishing attempt. Michael felt relieved and grateful that a simple habit—taking a moment to verify information—had protected him from potential fraud.

As his confidence grew, Michael started helping friends and family improve their security practices. He showed his parents how to enable multifactor authentication and explained why software updates mattered. He encouraged friends to use password managers and review privacy settings. Many were surprised to learn how much protection could be gained through relatively simple changes.

Months later, Michael's company experienced a security awareness campaign. Employees received simulated phishing emails designed to test their responses. While many coworkers clicked the links, Michael recognized the warning signs immediately. His habit of carefully evaluating messages had become second nature.

The exercise demonstrated an important lesson. Security awareness was not about intelligence or technical expertise. It was about consistent behavior. Michael had not become a cybersecurity expert. He had simply developed habits that reduced risk and improved decision-making.

As technology continued evolving, Michael encountered new applications, services, and devices. Yet the principles he learned remained valuable. He understood that technology would change, but human behavior would continue playing a central role in security. Strong habits provided protection regardless of which devices or platforms he used.

Several years later, Michael reflected on how much his perspective had changed. He no longer viewed cybersecurity as a complicated technical field reserved for specialists. Instead, he saw it as a collection of practical life skills. The same discipline used to manage finances, maintain health, or drive safely applied to digital security as well.

Most importantly, Michael realized that cybersecurity was not about achieving perfection. Mistakes would happen. New threats would emerge. Complete protection was impossible. However, strong habits dramatically reduced the likelihood of becoming a victim and improved his ability to respond when challenges arose.

The small changes he implemented–strong passwords, multifactor authentication, software updates, cautious communication practices, and privacy awareness–had become routine parts of daily life. Individually, each habit provided modest benefits. Together, they formed a powerful security foundation.

Michael often shared one piece of advice with others: cybersecurity begins with habits. Expensive software, advanced devices, and sophisticated tools can help, but consistent behavior remains the most effective defense. Every secure decision strengthens protection, and every good habit contributes to long-term resilience.

His journey demonstrated that anyone can improve their security. No specialized training, advanced degrees, or technical certifications were required. All it took was awareness, commitment, and a willingness to develop habits that support safer digital behavior. In an increasingly connected world, those habits became some of the most valuable investments he ever made.

Chapter 4

Passwords, Passkeys, and Multifactor Authentication

In the modern digital world, access to your personal information is often controlled by a single factor: identity verification. Whether you are logging into email accounts, banking applications, social media platforms, cloud storage services, shopping websites, healthcare portals, or business systems, each service must determine whether you are truly the authorized user. This process is known as authentication. While authentication may seem like a simple step in daily technology use, it represents one of the most important foundations of cybersecurity. If attackers can successfully impersonate you, they may gain access to your most valuable information. Understanding passwords, passkeys, and multifactor authentication is therefore essential for protecting your digital life.

For decades, passwords have served as the primary method of authentication. A password is a secret piece of information known only to the user and the service being accessed. When entered correctly, the system grants access. In theory, passwords are a simple and effective security solution. In practice, however, human behavior often weakens their effectiveness. Many people choose passwords that are easy to remember but also easy to guess. Others reuse the same password across multiple accounts, creating opportunities for widespread compromise if a single account is breached.

Cybercriminals understand these weaknesses and actively exploit them. One common attack method is known as credential stuffing. When a company experiences a data breach, attackers often obtain lists of usernames and passwords. They then test those credentials against other websites and services. If users have reused passwords, attackers may gain access to multiple accounts using a single stolen credential. This technique has been responsible for millions of account compromises worldwide.

Another common attack involves password guessing. Many users rely on predictable passwords that include names, birthdays, pet names, sports teams, or simple number sequences. Automated tools can rapidly test thousands or even millions of common password combinations. Weak passwords often fall within seconds. Longer and more complex passwords significantly increase resistance to these attacks.

A strong password should be unique, difficult to predict, and used only for a single account. Length is often more important than complexity alone. A password consisting of multiple unrelated words may provide stronger protection than a short password filled with symbols. For example, a random phrase containing several unrelated words can be easier to remember while remaining highly resistant to guessing attacks. The goal is to create credentials that attackers cannot easily predict or generate.

Managing numerous strong passwords can be challenging. Most individuals maintain dozens or even hundreds of online accounts. Remembering unique credentials for each service quickly becomes impractical. Password managers solve this problem by securely storing login credentials in an encrypted vault. Users only need to remember one master password while the manager generates and stores strong credentials for individual accounts. Password managers also reduce the temptation to reuse passwords across multiple services.

Despite their importance, passwords have limitations. They can be stolen through phishing attacks, malware infections, data breaches, social engineering, or accidental disclosure. Even strong passwords become vulnerable if attackers obtain them through alternative methods. This reality has led cybersecurity professionals to promote additional layers of authentication beyond passwords alone.

Multifactor authentication, often abbreviated as MFA, provides one of the most effective security improvements available. MFA requires users to present two or more forms of verification before access is granted. These factors typically fall into three categories: something you know, something you have, and something you are. A password represents something you know. A smartphone or security key represents something you have. A fingerprint or facial scan represents something you are.

When MFA is enabled, attackers who obtain a password still face additional barriers. For example, after entering a password, a user may receive a temporary code on a trusted device. Without access to that device, attackers cannot complete the login process. This significantly reduces the effectiveness of stolen credentials. Numerous studies have shown that MFA prevents a large percentage of account compromise attempts.

Several forms of MFA exist. Text message verification codes remain common, although they are not the strongest option. Authentication applications generate temporary codes directly on a trusted device and generally provide greater security. Hardware security keys offer even stronger protection by requiring physical possession of a dedicated authentication device. Biometric authentication methods such as fingerprints and facial recognition can also serve as additional factors.

Biometric authentication has become increasingly popular due to its convenience. Modern smartphones allow users to unlock devices and authorize transactions using fingerprints or facial recognition. While biometrics provide a useful security layer, they should not be viewed as perfect solutions. Environmental conditions, hardware limitations, and advanced attack methods may occasionally affect reliability. Biometrics work best when combined with other authentication factors.

A newer authentication technology known as passkeys is beginning to transform account security. Passkeys are designed to replace traditional passwords with cryptographic authentication methods. Instead of requiring users to remember passwords, passkeys use secure digital credentials stored on trusted devices. Authentication occurs through biometrics, device verification, or other secure methods. Passkeys are highly resistant to phishing attacks because there is no password for attackers to steal.

One of the most significant advantages of passkeys is their simplicity. Users no longer need to create, remember, or manage complex passwords. The authentication process becomes both more secure and more convenient. As major technology companies continue adopting passkey standards, passwordless authentication is expected to become increasingly common across digital services.

Phishing remains one of the greatest threats to authentication security. Cybercriminals frequently create fake login pages designed to capture credentials. These pages often closely resemble legitimate websites, making them difficult to distinguish from authentic services. Users should carefully verify website addresses before entering login information and avoid clicking links in unexpected messages. Even strong passwords provide little protection if voluntarily entered into fraudulent websites.

Account recovery mechanisms also deserve attention. Many services allow users to recover access through email addresses, phone numbers, or security questions. Weak recovery methods can undermine otherwise strong security practices. Recovery options should be secured with the same level of care applied to primary authentication methods. A compromised recovery account can provide attackers with indirect access to multiple services.

Organizations increasingly encourage users to adopt stronger authentication practices because account compromise remains one of the most common causes of security incidents. Whether the target is a personal email account or a corporate system, attackers frequently focus on authentication weaknesses because they often provide the easiest path to valuable information.

The future of authentication will likely involve a combination of biometrics, passkeys, hardware security devices, and advanced cryptographic systems. While technology continues evolving, the underlying principle remains consistent: verifying identity accurately while preventing unauthorized access. The goal is to make authentication both secure and convenient enough for widespread adoption.

Users who invest time in strengthening authentication practices dramatically reduce their exposure to cyber threats. Strong passwords, password managers, multifactor authentication, secure recovery methods, and passkey adoption collectively create a powerful defense against account compromise. Because so much of modern life depends on digital accounts, protecting authentication credentials should be considered one of the highest cybersecurity priorities.

Ultimately, cybersecurity often begins at the login screen. Every account, application, service, and system relies on authentication as its first line of defense. By understanding how passwords, passkeys, and multifactor authentication work, users gain the knowledge needed to protect their identities, secure their accounts, and maintain control over their digital lives.

How were attackers finding her accounts?

Sophia considered herself careful with technology. She paid bills online, stored important documents in cloud services, managed investments through mobile applications, and communicated with family and coworkers through digital platforms. Like many people, she used passwords for dozens of accounts but rarely thought much about them beyond remembering how to log in.

One evening, Sophia received an email from a social media platform notifying her of unusual login activity. According to the message, someone had attempted to access her account from another country. Although the login attempt had failed, the incident made her uneasy. She immediately changed her password and assumed the problem was resolved.

A few weeks later, a second notification arrived from an unrelated service. This time, someone had successfully logged into an old shopping account she had not used in years. While no financial damage occurred, the event raised concerns. How were attackers finding her accounts?

Determined to understand the situation, Sophia began researching cybersecurity. She quickly discovered an uncomfortable truth: she had been reusing variations of the same password across numerous services for years. If one password became exposed through a data breach, attackers could potentially access multiple accounts.

The realization was alarming. Sophia decided to take action. She installed a reputable password manager and began replacing old passwords with unique, randomly generated credentials. The process took several days because she maintained far more accounts than she initially realized. Banking platforms, streaming services, social media accounts, email providers, healthcare portals, shopping websites, and countless applications all required updates.

During her research, Sophia also learned about multifactor authentication. Although she had seen prompts encouraging activation, she had always considered them inconvenient. After reading numerous case studies involving compromised accounts, she changed her mind. She enabled MFA wherever possible, starting with her email account because it served as a recovery method for many other services.

Several months later, Sophia experienced the value of these changes firsthand. One afternoon, she received an authentication notification on her smartphone requesting approval for a login attempt. The request had not originated from her. Someone had apparently obtained one of her passwords and attempted to access an account.

Because MFA was enabled, the attacker could not proceed without the second verification factor. Sophia denied the request, changed the account password, and reviewed recent activity. No unauthorized access had occurred. What could have become a serious incident ended as a minor inconvenience.

Encouraged by this experience, Sophia continued strengthening her security practices. She began using passkeys whenever services offered the option. Initially unfamiliar with the technology, she appreciated how simple the process became. Instead of remembering passwords, authentication relied on secure device verification and biometric confirmation.

As her confidence grew, Sophia shared what she learned with her family. Her father admitted using the same password for nearly every account. Her younger brother relied on weak credentials because he believed hackers only targeted wealthy individuals. Sophia explained that cybercriminals often target ordinary users precisely because they tend to have weaker defenses.

Together, they upgraded passwords, enabled MFA, and reviewed account recovery settings. What started as a personal security project evolved into a family effort to improve digital protection. The process sparked conversations about privacy, identity theft, and the importance of proactive security.

Months later, Sophia attended a cybersecurity conference hosted by her employer. During a presentation, a speaker described authentication as the front door to the digital world. The analogy resonated with her. Just as people lock their homes and secure valuable possessions, they must also protect access to their digital lives. A single compromised account can open pathways to countless other systems and services.

The presentation reinforced lessons Sophia had already experienced firsthand. Authentication was not merely a technical concept. It was a fundamental safeguard protecting finances, communications, personal memories, professional opportunities, and identity itself. Every account represented a doorway, and every password or passkey served as a key.

Years passed, and technology continued evolving. Passkeys became increasingly common. Biometric authentication improved. New security standards emerged. Yet the principles

Sophia learned remained relevant. Strong authentication protected accounts regardless of how underlying technologies changed.

Occasionally, friends would ask how she managed to avoid many of the security problems they encountered. Her answer was always simple. She focused on protecting the entry points. Strong passwords, password managers, multifactor authentication, passkeys, and secure recovery settings formed the foundation of her cybersecurity strategy.

Sophia understood that no security measure could guarantee complete protection. Attackers would continue developing new techniques, and technology would continue changing. However, she also knew that strengthening authentication dramatically reduced risk. Every layer added another obstacle for attackers to overcome.

Looking back, Sophia was grateful for those early warning notifications that had prompted her to take action. What initially seemed like minor inconveniences ultimately led her to adopt habits that protected her digital life for years to come. The experience taught her an important lesson: cybersecurity often begins with something as simple as a login screen.

By protecting authentication, she protected everything built upon it. Her accounts remained secure, her information remained private, and her confidence in navigating the digital world continued growing. The lessons she learned would remain valuable regardless of what technologies emerged in the future because identity verification would always remain at the heart of cybersecurity.

For Sophia, passwords, passkeys, and multifactor authentication were no longer technical terms. They were practical tools that helped safeguard her identity, her information, and her future in an increasingly connected world.

Chapter 5

Securing Your Smartphone Against Physical Theft and Loss

When most people think about cybersecurity, they imagine hackers operating behind computer screens, malware infecting devices through the internet, or cybercriminals stealing information through sophisticated attacks. While these threats are important, one of the most common security risks remains surprisingly simple: physical access to a smartphone. A lost, misplaced, or stolen device can expose enormous amounts of personal information if proper security measures are not in place. Because smartphones contain access to financial accounts, emails, social media platforms, personal photos, business documents, passwords, and sensitive communications, physical security should be considered an essential component of mobile cybersecurity.

Modern smartphones serve as digital extensions of their owners. In many cases, they contain years of personal history. Family photographs, banking records, health information, work-related documents, location histories, messages, contacts, and cloud account access may all reside within a single device. A criminal who gains physical possession of an unsecured smartphone may obtain direct access to valuable information or use the device as a stepping stone to compromise additional accounts.

One of the most important security measures users can implement is enabling a strong screen lock. A screen lock serves as the first barrier protecting a smartphone from unauthorized access. Without a lock screen, anyone who picks up a device can immediately access its contents. Modern smartphones offer several authentication options, including PIN codes, passwords, fingerprints, and facial recognition systems. While each method has advantages, combining convenience with security is essential. Weak PINs such as 1234, 0000, or birth years should be avoided because they can often be guessed quickly.

Longer passcodes generally provide stronger protection. Many modern devices allow users to create six-digit or longer PINs as well as full passwords. While slightly less convenient than short codes, stronger credentials significantly increase resistance to unauthorized access. The small inconvenience of entering a longer code is minimal compared to the potential consequences of data exposure.

Biometric authentication technologies have become increasingly common. Fingerprint readers and facial recognition systems provide fast and convenient access while maintaining strong security. These systems help encourage users to keep lock screens enabled because authentication becomes quick and seamless. Although no biometric system is perfect, they offer substantial improvements compared to leaving devices unprotected.

Automatic locking features are equally important. Smartphones should be configured to lock automatically after short periods of inactivity. Many users disable automatic locking because they find repeated authentication inconvenient. Unfortunately, an unlocked device left unattended even briefly can create opportunities for unauthorized access. Automatic locking reduces this risk by ensuring that devices secure themselves when not actively being used.

Device encryption provides another critical layer of protection. Encryption converts stored information into unreadable data that can only be accessed using proper authentication credentials. Most modern smartphones enable encryption automatically when security features are activated. If a device is stolen, encryption helps prevent attackers from extracting information directly from storage systems. Without encryption, sophisticated attackers may be able to recover data even if a lock screen is present.

Location tracking services play an important role in device recovery. Both Android and iPhone platforms offer features that allow users to locate lost devices, display messages on lock screens, trigger alarms, and remotely erase information if necessary. These tools can significantly improve the chances of recovering a lost smartphone while also reducing the risk of unauthorized access. Users should verify that device tracking services are enabled before problems occur.

Remote wipe capabilities provide valuable protection when recovery is unlikely. If a smartphone is lost or stolen and cannot be recovered, remote wipe functions allow users to erase sensitive information from a distance. While losing a device can be frustrating, losing both the device and the information it contains can be far more damaging. Remote wiping helps protect personal information even when physical recovery is impossible.

Backup systems become especially important in theft and loss scenarios. Individuals who maintain current backups can replace a lost device and restore important information relatively quickly. Those without backups may permanently lose photos, contacts, messages, documents, and other valuable data. Effective cybersecurity involves both protecting information from unauthorized access and ensuring it remains available when needed.

Public environments often present elevated theft risks. Airports, hotels, restaurants, public transportation systems, conferences, sporting events, and shopping centers are common locations for smartphone theft. Criminals frequently target distracted individuals who leave devices unattended or fail to notice suspicious activity. Maintaining awareness of surroundings and keeping devices secured reduces opportunities for theft.

Travel introduces additional security considerations. Tourists often rely heavily on smartphones for navigation, communication, payments, and travel management. Unfortunately, unfamiliar environments can increase vulnerability to theft. Travelers should understand local risks, maintain backups, secure devices appropriately, and avoid displaying valuable electronics unnecessarily in high-risk areas.

Many users underestimate the risks associated with temporary physical access. A smartphone does not necessarily need to be stolen to be compromised. An individual who gains access to a device for only a few minutes may install malicious applications, modify settings, access sensitive information, or alter account configurations. Protecting devices from unauthorized access at all times is therefore important, even in trusted environments.

Social engineering can also play a role in physical theft. Criminals may create distractions, impersonate authority figures, or exploit trust to gain access to devices. Understanding these tactics helps users recognize suspicious situations before problems occur. Security awareness should extend beyond digital threats to include real-world interactions that may affect device safety.

Children and family members may unintentionally create security risks if devices are shared without proper safeguards. Family sharing practices should include awareness of privacy settings, application permissions, and account security. While sharing devices may sometimes be necessary, appropriate controls help maintain protection.

Organizations frequently implement strict policies regarding mobile device security because lost or stolen devices can expose sensitive business information. Employees who access corporate resources through personal smartphones should understand organizational security requirements and follow established guidelines. Personal security practices often contribute directly to broader organizational security.

Many smartphone thefts are crimes of opportunity. Attackers often target devices that appear easy to steal or access. Visible security measures such as lock screens, tracking capabilities, and strong authentication increase the effort required to exploit stolen devices. Criminals generally prefer easier targets when available.

Preparation remains one of the most effective defenses. Users should know what actions to take if a device is lost or stolen. Important steps may include locating the device, locking it remotely, changing account passwords, contacting service providers, monitoring financial accounts, and reporting theft to authorities when appropriate. Having a response plan reduces panic and improves decision-making during stressful situations.

Physical security and cybersecurity are closely connected. A secure smartphone protects not only the device itself but also the information, accounts, and services connected to it. Users who neglect physical security may inadvertently undermine otherwise strong cybersecurity practices. Effective protection requires attention to both digital and physical threats.

Ultimately, smartphones represent significant investments in both technology and information. Protecting them from theft and loss is not simply about preserving hardware; it is about safeguarding identities, relationships, finances, memories, and opportunities. Strong physical security habits complement digital defenses and contribute to a comprehensive approach to mobile protection.

Ethan stopped at a busy café after work

Ethan considered himself careful with technology. He used strong passwords, enabled multifactor authentication, updated software regularly, and followed cybersecurity news. Friends often came to him for advice about protecting online accounts and avoiding scams. Yet despite his awareness of digital threats, he rarely thought about physical device security.

One afternoon, Ethan stopped at a busy café after work. He placed his smartphone on the table beside his laptop while responding to emails and reviewing documents. The environment felt comfortable and familiar. Customers moved in and out continuously, conversations filled the room, and employees prepared drinks behind the counter.

At some point, Ethan became distracted by an urgent work call. When the conversation ended, he reached for his phone and discovered it was gone. At first, he assumed he had misplaced it. He checked his bag, searched nearby tables, and retraced his steps. The realization gradually set in: the device had likely been stolen.

Panic quickly followed. Ethan's smartphone contained years of personal photos, financial applications, business communications, and access to numerous online accounts. Although he had prepared for many cybersecurity threats, he had never seriously considered the possibility of losing physical possession of the device.

Fortunately, Ethan had enabled several security features. Using a friend's computer, he logged into his account and accessed the device tracking service. The map displayed the phone's last known location several miles away. He immediately activated lost mode, locking the device remotely and displaying a message requesting its return.

Over the next several hours, Ethan monitored the situation carefully. The device continued moving throughout the city. Recovery seemed increasingly unlikely. Recognizing the risk, he activated the remote wipe function to erase sensitive information. Although disappointed to lose the device, he felt relieved knowing that personal data would remain protected.

The following day, Ethan reviewed his accounts. Multifactor authentication prevented unauthorized access even if someone managed to obtain information from the phone. Banking applications remained secure. Email accounts showed no suspicious activity. Cloud services remained protected. His preparation had significantly reduced potential damage.

While waiting for a replacement device, Ethan reflected on the experience. He realized that physical theft could be just as disruptive as many cyberattacks. A stolen smartphone represented more than the loss of hardware. It threatened access to personal information, financial resources, professional responsibilities, and daily routines.

Several weeks later, Ethan attended a community cybersecurity seminar and shared his story. Participants were surprised by how quickly an ordinary situation had become a security incident. Many admitted they rarely used screen locks, had never configured device tracking services, or lacked recent backups.

Ethan explained how specific security measures had protected him. The lock screen prevented immediate access. Encryption safeguarded stored information. Tracking services provided visibility. Remote wipe capabilities eliminated remaining risks. Backups allowed him to restore data onto a replacement device with minimal disruption. None of these measures were complicated, yet together they proved invaluable.

Inspired by the discussion, several attendees implemented security improvements on their own devices. Some enabled multifactor authentication for the first time. Others configured location tracking or reviewed backup settings. The group realized that preparation before an incident mattered far more than reacting afterward.

Months later, Ethan encountered another reminder of the importance of physical security. While traveling through an airport, he noticed a passenger leave a smartphone unattended at a charging station. Within minutes, someone picked up the device and walked away. Whether the individual intended to return it or keep it remained unclear, but the situation illustrated how quickly opportunities arise.

The experience reinforced Ethan's belief that security requires both awareness and preparation. Technology provides powerful tools, but users must choose to activate and maintain them. Waiting until after a theft occurs often limits available options.

Over time, Ethan became an advocate for comprehensive mobile security. He emphasized that protecting smartphones involves much more than avoiding hackers. Physical theft, accidental loss, and unauthorized access can be equally damaging. Effective security addresses all potential threats rather than focusing exclusively on digital attacks.

Looking back, Ethan considered himself fortunate. Although losing his smartphone was inconvenient and stressful, the incident could have been far worse. Strong preparation transformed what might have become a major crisis into a manageable problem. His data remained secure, his accounts remained protected, and his digital life continued with minimal disruption.

Most importantly, the experience changed how he viewed cybersecurity. He no longer separated physical security from digital security. Both worked together to protect the same valuable assets. A secure smartphone required strong authentication, updated software, privacy controls, backups, and physical protection. Neglecting any one area could weaken the entire system.

Ethan often summarized the lesson in a simple statement: protecting a smartphone means protecting everything connected to it. The device itself may be small enough to fit in a pocket, but the information it contains can represent an entire digital life. Safeguarding that life requires preparation, awareness, and consistent security habits that extend beyond the screen and into the physical world.

From that day forward, Ethan never left a device unattended, always verified backup status, and regularly reviewed recovery settings. The habits became second nature, providing peace of mind whenever he traveled, worked, or went about daily life. The stolen phone had taught him a valuable lesson—one that would continue protecting him for years to come.

Chapter 6

Software Updates, Security Patches, and Why They Matter

One of the simplest yet most important actions smartphone users can take to improve security is keeping their devices updated. While software updates may seem like routine maintenance or minor improvements, they play a critical role in protecting devices from cyber threats. Every year, software developers discover thousands of vulnerabilities that could potentially be exploited by cybercriminals. Security patches and software updates are designed to correct these weaknesses before attackers can take advantage of them. Users who understand the importance of updates and develop consistent update habits significantly reduce their exposure to digital threats.

To understand why updates matter, it is important to first understand vulnerabilities. A vulnerability is a weakness, flaw, or mistake within software that could allow unauthorized actions to occur. Vulnerabilities may exist within operating systems, mobile applications, web browsers, communication services, or even hardware components. Software systems are extremely complex, often containing millions of lines of code written by thousands of developers over many years. Despite extensive testing, mistakes occasionally occur, and vulnerabilities are sometimes discovered after products are released.

Cybercriminals actively search for vulnerabilities because they provide opportunities to bypass security protections. A vulnerability may allow attackers to steal information, install malware, gain unauthorized access, spy on users, or disrupt normal device operation. Once a vulnerability becomes publicly known, attackers often begin developing methods to exploit it as quickly as possible. This creates a race between software developers releasing fixes and attackers attempting to take advantage of unprotected systems.

Security patches are software updates specifically designed to fix vulnerabilities. When developers discover weaknesses, they create patches that modify software behavior and eliminate opportunities for exploitation. Once the patch is released, users must install it for protection to take effect. Simply making a patch available does not automatically secure every device. Protection depends on users applying updates promptly.

Operating system updates are among the most important security updates available. Mobile operating systems such as Android and iOS manage core device functions and enforce security controls. Vulnerabilities within operating systems can potentially affect every application and service running on a device. Because operating systems control access to sensitive resources, attackers often focus significant effort on identifying weaknesses within them. Keeping operating systems current helps ensure that known vulnerabilities are addressed before they can be exploited.

Application updates are equally important. Many users focus on operating system updates while neglecting individual applications. However, applications frequently process sensitive information such as financial data, personal communications, and authentication credentials. Vulnerabilities within apps may create opportunities for attackers even if the underlying operating system remains secure. Regular application updates help maintain protection across the entire device ecosystem.

One reason some users delay updates is fear of inconvenience. Updates occasionally require device restarts, consume storage space, or temporarily interrupt normal activities. While these concerns are understandable, the security benefits almost always outweigh the inconvenience. A brief interruption caused by an update is generally preferable to the consequences of a successful cyberattack or data breach.

Another common misconception is that older devices are less attractive targets. Some users assume attackers focus exclusively on the newest technology. In reality, outdated devices often become more attractive targets because they may lack critical security updates. Cybercriminals frequently search for systems running older software versions because known vulnerabilities may remain unpatched. Unsupported devices can present significant security risks if no further updates are available.

The concept of zero-day vulnerabilities highlights the importance of timely updates. A zero-day vulnerability is a flaw that becomes known before a patch is available. Because no fix exists initially, attackers may have an opportunity to exploit affected systems. Once developers release a patch, users should install it as quickly as possible to close the vulnerability. Delayed updates prolong exposure and increase risk.

Automatic updates provide one of the most effective solutions for maintaining security. Most modern smartphones offer options to install updates automatically. Automatic updates reduce the likelihood of users forgetting or postponing important security improvements. While manual updates provide greater control, automatic systems often ensure more consistent protection.

Software updates frequently include improvements beyond security. Developers may enhance performance, improve stability, introduce new features, optimize battery life, and resolve software bugs. While these benefits are valuable, security remains one of the most important reasons to maintain current software. Many updates contain security enhancements that users may never notice directly but that provide significant protection behind the scenes.

Enterprise environments provide useful examples of the importance of updates. Organizations invest substantial resources in patch management because unpatched systems frequently contribute to security incidents. A single vulnerable device can sometimes create risks for entire networks. The same principle applies to personal devices. An unpatched smartphone may expose not only the user but also family members, employers, and others connected through shared services.

Application stores play an important role in update distribution. Official app stores provide centralized mechanisms for delivering security fixes and software improvements. Users who download applications from trusted sources benefit from streamlined update processes and additional security screening. Installing software from unofficial sources may increase the risk of missing critical updates or receiving malicious software disguised as legitimate applications.

Users should also pay attention to update notifications rather than dismissing them indefinitely. While it may be tempting to postpone updates repeatedly, doing so extends vulnerability windows. Attackers often monitor update releases closely because patches sometimes reveal information about previously undisclosed weaknesses. Once details become public, exploitation attempts may increase rapidly.

Firmware updates deserve attention as well. Firmware controls low-level hardware operations and may affect security-sensitive components. Manufacturers occasionally release firmware updates to address vulnerabilities, improve performance, or enhance functionality. Although less visible than application updates, firmware updates can play an important role in overall device security.

Security researchers, technology companies, and government agencies regularly encourage prompt patching because it remains one of the most effective cybersecurity practices available. Unlike some security measures that require extensive technical knowledge, installing updates is relatively simple. Yet the protection provided can be substantial.

Users should understand that cybersecurity is not a static condition. Threats evolve continuously. New vulnerabilities emerge, attackers develop new techniques, and software ecosystems change over time. Updates allow devices to adapt to these evolving conditions. Without updates, security gradually deteriorates as known weaknesses accumulate.

The relationship between updates and risk management is straightforward. Every unpatched vulnerability represents potential risk. Each applied patch reduces that risk. While no device can ever be completely secure, maintaining current software significantly improves resilience against known threats. Consistent updates help ensure that users benefit from the latest defensive technologies and security improvements.

Ultimately, software updates represent one of the easiest and most effective investments users can make in their cybersecurity. A few minutes spent installing updates can prevent data theft, malware infections, financial losses, and countless other security problems. By treating updates as a routine part of device maintenance, users strengthen their defenses and contribute to a safer digital environment.

Cybersecurity experts urged users to install patches immediately

Jason loved technology and enjoyed experimenting with new mobile applications. He used his smartphone for work, communication, banking, shopping, travel planning, and entertainment. Whenever update notifications appeared, however, he usually ignored them. Updates seemed inconvenient, and he rarely noticed significant differences after installing them. As a result, he often postponed updates for weeks or even months.

One afternoon, Jason attended a cybersecurity awareness seminar organized by his employer. During the presentation, a security specialist discussed the role of software updates in preventing cyberattacks. The speaker explained how vulnerabilities are discovered, how patches are developed, and how attackers frequently target devices that remain unpatched.

Jason listened politely but remained skeptical. His phone appeared to work perfectly well without frequent updates. Why interrupt his routine for changes he could barely notice?

Several weeks later, news reports began covering a major mobile security vulnerability affecting millions of devices worldwide. The flaw allowed attackers to potentially gain unauthorized access under certain conditions. Technology companies quickly released security updates to address the issue. Cybersecurity experts urged users to install patches immediately.

Curious, Jason checked his device settings and discovered that the update containing the fix had been available for nearly two weeks. He had dismissed the notification multiple times without realizing its importance. For the first time, he began considering the possibility that updates might matter more than he previously believed.

That evening, he installed the update and started researching how software vulnerabilities work. He learned that many successful cyberattacks exploit weaknesses that developers have already fixed. In many cases, victims remain vulnerable simply because updates were never installed. The realization was eye-opening.

Motivated to improve his habits, Jason enabled automatic updates for both his operating system and applications. He also reviewed installed software and discovered several apps that had not been updated in months. Some included security fixes addressing known vulnerabilities. Gradually, he began viewing updates not as inconveniences but as routine maintenance similar to locking doors or servicing a vehicle.

Several months later, one of Jason's friends experienced a security incident involving an outdated application. The friend had ignored updates for an extended period and unknowingly continued using a version containing a publicly known vulnerability. Attackers exploited the weakness and gained access to sensitive information. While the damage was eventually contained, the experience reinforced lessons Jason had recently learned.

As time passed, Jason noticed additional benefits from maintaining current software. Applications became more stable, battery performance improved, and new features enhanced usability. While security remained his primary motivation, the overall user experience improved as well. Updates were no longer interruptions; they became opportunities to strengthen and optimize his device.

One day, Jason received a notification about a critical operating system update. Instead of postponing it, he installed it immediately. The process took only a few minutes. Later that week, cybersecurity news sources reported active exploitation attempts targeting the exact vulnerability addressed by the patch. Because he had updated promptly, Jason's device remained protected.

The incident demonstrated an important principle. Users often never realize how many attacks they avoid because security measures work quietly in the background. Successful protection rarely attracts attention. Yet every prevented compromise represents a significant victory.

As his understanding grew, Jason began helping family members maintain their devices as well. He assisted his parents in enabling automatic updates and explained why update notifications should not be ignored. He also encouraged coworkers to view patching as an essential security habit rather than an optional task.

Over time, Jason's attitude toward cybersecurity evolved significantly. He realized that strong security often depends on simple, consistent actions rather than advanced technical expertise. Installing updates required little effort, yet provided substantial protection against a wide range of threats.

Several years later, Jason reflected on how much his perspective had changed. What once seemed like annoying notifications had become valuable reminders to maintain security. He understood that software developers, security researchers, and technology companies invested enormous effort into identifying and correcting vulnerabilities. Installing updates allowed him to benefit from that collective work.

The experience taught Jason an enduring lesson: cybersecurity is often about reducing risk through consistent habits. No single update could guarantee complete protection, but every patch reduced opportunities for attackers. Small actions performed regularly created meaningful improvements over time.

Whenever friends complained about update notifications, Jason shared his story. He explained how vulnerabilities work, why patches matter, and how quickly attackers exploit known weaknesses. Most importantly, he emphasized that cybersecurity is not always about dramatic incidents or sophisticated defenses. Sometimes it is as simple as pressing the update button.

By adopting this mindset, Jason transformed one of the easiest cybersecurity practices into one of his strongest defenses. His devices remained current, vulnerabilities were addressed promptly, and he enjoyed greater confidence in the security of his digital life. The lesson was clear: software updates may seem ordinary, but their impact can be extraordinary.

In a world where cyber threats evolve constantly, staying updated became one of Jason's most valuable habits. Each patch represented another layer of protection, another obstacle for attackers, and another step toward a safer digital future. Through awareness, consistency, and a willingness to act, he turned a previously ignored task into a cornerstone of his cybersecurity strategy.

Chapter 7

Mobile Malware, Viruses, and How Infections Happen

One of the most widely discussed topics in cybersecurity is malware. The term malware is short for "malicious software" and refers to any software intentionally designed to harm devices, steal information, monitor activity, disrupt operations, or provide unauthorized access to attackers. While many people associate malware with traditional desktop computers, mobile devices have become increasingly attractive targets for cybercriminals. Smartphones now contain valuable personal and financial information, making them ideal targets for malicious activity. Understanding how mobile malware works, how infections occur, and how to prevent them is essential for every smartphone user.

Mobile malware has evolved significantly over the years. Early forms of mobile malware were relatively simple and limited in capability. As smartphones became more powerful and connected to more services, cybercriminals developed increasingly sophisticated threats. Modern malware can steal passwords, monitor communications, track locations, record keystrokes, intercept messages, access financial information, and even take control of certain device functions. In some cases, users may not realize their devices have been compromised until significant damage has already occurred.

One of the most important things to understand is that malware rarely appears without a cause. Most infections occur because attackers successfully convince users to install malicious software, click harmful links, approve dangerous permissions, or interact with fraudulent content. While software vulnerabilities can occasionally allow automatic infections, human behavior often plays a central role in the infection process. Understanding common infection methods helps users recognize risks before problems occur.

Malicious applications remain one of the most common infection sources. Attackers frequently create apps that appear legitimate but contain hidden malicious functionality. These applications may imitate popular games, utility tools, financial services, productivity software, or entertainment platforms. Once installed, malicious apps may request extensive permissions and begin collecting information without the user's knowledge. Some apps function normally while secretly performing harmful activities in the background.

Unofficial application stores present elevated risks because they may lack rigorous security screening processes. Official stores operated by major platform providers perform various checks designed to identify malicious software before distribution. While no system is perfect, official stores generally provide significantly greater protection than unknown third-party sources. Downloading applications only from trusted sources remains one of the most effective malware prevention strategies.

Phishing attacks often serve as malware delivery mechanisms. Cybercriminals send emails, text messages, social media messages, or advertisements containing links to malicious websites. These sites may encourage users to download fake security tools, software updates, financial applications, or other programs. Because the content appears legitimate, many victims install malware voluntarily without realizing the risk. Awareness and verification are essential defenses against these tactics.

Malicious advertisements, sometimes referred to as malvertising, represent another infection pathway. Attackers place harmful code within online advertisements that appear on websites or applications. Clicking these ads may redirect users to dangerous websites, trigger unwanted downloads, or expose them to additional scams. While advertising networks work to identify and remove malicious content, users should remain cautious when interacting with unfamiliar advertisements.

Trojans are among the most common forms of mobile malware. Named after the legendary Trojan Horse, these programs disguise themselves as legitimate software while secretly performing malicious actions. A Trojan may appear to be a useful utility, game, or productivity tool. Once installed, however, it may steal information, grant remote access to attackers, or download additional malware. The deceptive nature of Trojans makes them particularly dangerous.

Spyware is another significant threat category. Spyware is designed to monitor user activity and collect information without consent. It may record keystrokes, capture screenshots, monitor browsing activity, track locations, access communications, or gather personal information. Some spyware targets specific individuals, while other variants operate on a larger scale. Because spyware often functions silently, victims may remain unaware of its presence for extended periods.

Ransomware has also expanded into mobile environments. Mobile ransomware may lock devices, encrypt files, restrict access to applications, or display fraudulent warnings demanding payment. Attackers typically promise to restore access after receiving money, although victims are not guaranteed recovery. Preventive measures such as backups, cautious software installation, and regular updates remain the most effective defenses.

Banking malware specifically targets financial applications and transactions. These threats may intercept login credentials, capture authentication codes, manipulate transactions, or display fake login screens designed to steal information. Because mobile banking has become increasingly common, attackers view financial applications as highly valuable targets. Strong authentication, secure software practices, and careful verification help reduce these risks.

Rootkits represent a more advanced malware category. Rootkits are designed to gain deep control over operating systems while avoiding detection. Once installed, they may allow attackers to manipulate device behavior, conceal malicious activities, and maintain long-term access. Although less common than other malware types, rootkits can be particularly difficult to detect and remove.

Signs of malware infection vary depending on the threat involved. Common indicators may include unexpected battery drain, unusual data usage, excessive device heating, slow performance, unfamiliar applications, unauthorized account activity, intrusive advertisements, frequent crashes, or unusual system behavior. While these symptoms do not always indicate malware, they should encourage users to investigate potential issues.

Security updates play an important role in malware prevention because they address vulnerabilities attackers may exploit. Outdated software often provides easier opportunities for malware installation and operation. Maintaining current operating systems and applications reduces exposure to known threats. Updates should therefore be viewed as proactive security measures rather than optional maintenance tasks.

Application permissions deserve careful attention. Many malware infections become more damaging because users grant excessive permissions. A malicious app with access to contacts, storage, location data, cameras, microphones, and messages can collect substantial information. Reviewing permissions before installation and periodically auditing existing apps helps limit potential damage.

Mobile security solutions can provide additional protection. Antivirus applications, security monitoring tools, and threat detection services may identify suspicious behavior and warn users about known threats. While these tools should not replace good security habits, they can complement broader security strategies.

The best defense against malware combines awareness, caution, and proactive security practices. Users should download apps from trusted sources, avoid suspicious links, maintain current software, review permissions carefully, enable security features, and remain informed about emerging threats. Malware prevention is often easier and less costly than recovering from an infection.

Understanding how infections occur transforms malware from a mysterious threat into a manageable risk. While no device can be completely immune to attack, informed users significantly reduce their chances of becoming victims. Knowledge, vigilance, and responsible behavior remain among the most effective cybersecurity tools available.

Ultimately, mobile malware represents an evolving challenge rather than an unavoidable fate. Attackers continually develop new techniques, but users who understand how malware works are far better equipped to recognize, avoid, and respond to potential threats. Awareness remains the foundation of effective defense.

Daniel noticed an advertisement promoting a free application

Daniel relied heavily on his smartphone. It managed his schedule, stored important documents, handled financial transactions, connected him with family and friends, and served as his primary source of information throughout the day. Because he considered himself reasonably tech-savvy, he rarely worried about cybersecurity threats.

One evening, Daniel noticed an advertisement promoting a free application that promised to improve smartphone performance dramatically. The app claimed it could boost battery life, increase speed, free storage space, and provide advanced optimization features. Thousands of positive reviews accompanied the advertisement, making it appear trustworthy.

Without conducting much research, Daniel downloaded and installed the application. Initially, everything seemed normal. The app displayed colorful graphics, performed scans, and generated reports showing various optimizations. Daniel felt satisfied with his decision.

A few days later, however, strange things began happening. His battery drained unusually quickly. Data usage increased significantly even though his habits had not changed.

Advertisements appeared unexpectedly while using unrelated applications. The phone occasionally became warm even when idle.

Daniel initially dismissed these issues as minor glitches. Yet the problems continued worsening. Performance slowed noticeably. Certain applications crashed unexpectedly. Notifications appeared from services he had never used. Most concerning of all, he received alerts about login attempts involving several online accounts.

Concerned, Daniel began investigating. He reviewed recently installed applications and quickly noticed that the optimization app requested extensive permissions. It had access to storage, contacts, location services, and network communications. Research revealed that other users had reported similar issues. The application was widely suspected of containing malicious components.

Realizing the potential seriousness of the situation, Daniel immediately removed the application and installed a reputable mobile security tool. The scan identified multiple suspicious activities associated with the software. Fortunately, no major financial damage had occurred, but the experience served as a powerful wake-up call.

Determined to understand what happened, Daniel spent several weeks studying mobile malware and cybersecurity fundamentals. He learned how attackers disguise malicious software as legitimate applications. He discovered how excessive permissions can enable data collection and surveillance. Most importantly, he realized that infections often occur because users unknowingly trust the wrong software.

As Daniel's knowledge grew, so did his security practices. He began downloading apps exclusively from trusted sources. Before installing software, he researched developers, reviewed permissions, and examined user feedback carefully. He also enabled stronger security settings and updated applications regularly.

Several months later, Daniel received a text message claiming that a package delivery required immediate action. The message included a link and encouraged him to install a tracking application. Remembering lessons from his earlier experience, he became suspicious. Instead of clicking the link, he contacted the shipping company directly.

The company confirmed that no package existed and that the message was fraudulent. The link would have directed him to a malicious website designed to distribute malware. Daniel felt grateful that awareness had prevented him from repeating past mistakes.

Over time, Daniel became increasingly interested in cybersecurity. He followed security news, learned about emerging threats, and shared information with friends and family. Many were surprised to discover how common mobile malware had become. Some assumed smartphones were naturally immune to serious infections. Daniel explained that while modern devices include strong protections, user behavior remains an essential factor.

One weekend, Daniel helped his parents review applications installed on their devices. Together, they removed several unused apps, updated software, reviewed permissions, and enabled additional security features. The process revealed how easily potentially risky applications can accumulate over time.

Years later, Daniel often reflected on the optimization app that had started his cybersecurity journey. Although the experience had been frustrating, it ultimately provided valuable lessons. He learned that convenience should never replace caution and that every application deserves scrutiny before installation.

Most importantly, Daniel realized that malware prevention depends largely on informed decision-making. Cybercriminals often succeed by exploiting trust, curiosity, and convenience.

Users who understand these tactics are far less likely to become victims.

His smartphone eventually became one of the most secure devices among his friends and family. Strong authentication, regular updates, careful application management, and healthy skepticism created multiple layers of protection. While he understood that no security strategy could guarantee complete immunity, he felt confident in his ability to recognize and avoid many common threats.

Daniel frequently summarized his experience with a simple lesson: malware rarely appears by magic. Most infections begin with a decision. Whether clicking a link, installing an application, or granting permissions, users often play a role in determining their own risk. By making informed decisions, individuals can dramatically improve their security.

The incident that once seemed like an unfortunate mistake became one of the most valuable learning experiences of his life. It taught him that cybersecurity is not merely about technology. It is about awareness, responsibility, and understanding how attackers operate. Those lessons continued protecting him long after the malicious application had been removed.

As new malware threats emerged and technology continued evolving, Daniel remained prepared. His knowledge provided confidence, and his habits provided protection. Together, they formed a powerful defense against one of the most persistent challenges in the digital world: malicious software designed to exploit the unwary.

Through experience, education, and vigilance, Daniel transformed from a potential victim into a knowledgeable defender of his own digital life. That transformation began with a single lesson: understanding how infections happen is the first step toward preventing them.

Chapter 8

Recognizing and Avoiding Mobile Phishing, Smishing, and Social Engineering Attacks

Among all cybersecurity threats facing smartphone users today, phishing and social engineering attacks remain some of the most successful and dangerous. Unlike malware attacks that target software vulnerabilities or technical weaknesses, phishing attacks target people. Cybercriminals understand that human trust, curiosity, fear, urgency, and emotions can often be easier to exploit than technology itself. As smartphones become increasingly integrated into daily life, attackers continue refining techniques designed to deceive users into revealing information, granting access, or taking actions that compromise security.

Phishing is a type of cyberattack in which criminals impersonate trusted organizations, individuals, or services to trick victims into providing sensitive information. Attackers may pretend to be banks, government agencies, employers, delivery companies, social media platforms, online retailers, healthcare providers, or even friends and family members. The objective is usually to steal passwords, financial information, authentication codes, personal data, or account access credentials.

While phishing originally focused on email messages, mobile devices have expanded the attack surface considerably. Smartphones provide multiple communication channels that attackers can exploit, including text messages, messaging applications, social media platforms, collaboration tools, phone calls, and mobile notifications. These channels allow attackers to reach victims quickly and often create a sense of urgency that encourages immediate action.

Smishing is one of the fastest-growing forms of mobile phishing. The term combines SMS and phishing. In a smishing attack, criminals send fraudulent text messages designed to trick recipients into clicking malicious links, downloading harmful software, calling fake support numbers, or revealing sensitive information. Because text messages often appear more personal and urgent than emails, many users are more likely to trust them.

Common smishing messages involve package delivery notifications, banking alerts, account verification requests, unpaid toll notices, tax refunds, prize winnings, employment opportunities, subscription renewals, and security warnings. Attackers carefully craft messages to appear legitimate and often use logos, branding, and language that closely resemble trusted organizations. The goal is to lower suspicion and encourage immediate responses.

Email phishing remains highly effective despite widespread awareness. Cybercriminals continuously improve the quality of fraudulent emails. Modern phishing messages may contain professional graphics, realistic branding, convincing language, and links that appear legitimate at first glance. Attackers often study their targets and customize messages based on publicly available information, making attacks more believable.

Social media phishing has become increasingly common as users share more personal information online. Attackers may create fake profiles, impersonate trusted contacts, or send messages containing malicious links. Because messages appear to originate from familiar individuals or organizations, victims may lower their guard. Social media platforms provide attackers with valuable information that can be used to personalize scams and increase credibility.

Voice phishing, commonly known as vishing, involves fraudulent phone calls. Attackers may impersonate banks, technical support representatives, law enforcement officials, government agencies, or customer service personnel. They often create urgency by claiming that accounts have been compromised, payments are overdue, or legal action is pending. The goal is to pressure victims into revealing information before they have time to think critically.

One of the most powerful tools attackers use is emotional manipulation. Social engineering relies heavily on psychological principles. Fear is commonly used to trigger panic and urgency. Excitement may be used through promises of prizes, rewards, or financial opportunities. Curiosity can be exploited through unexpected notifications or messages. Trust is leveraged by impersonating familiar organizations or individuals. Understanding these emotional triggers helps users recognize manipulation attempts before they succeed.

Urgency is one of the most reliable indicators of phishing activity. Legitimate organizations rarely demand immediate action without providing alternative communication options. Messages that threaten account suspension, legal consequences, financial penalties, or service disruptions unless immediate action is taken should be viewed with caution. Attackers create urgency because rushed decisions reduce careful evaluation.

Links deserve special scrutiny. Many phishing attacks rely on directing victims to fraudulent websites that closely imitate legitimate services. These websites may appear nearly identical to authentic login pages. Users should examine website addresses carefully before entering credentials. Even small differences in spelling, domain names, or formatting can indicate fraudulent activity. Whenever possible, users should navigate directly to official websites rather than relying on links received through messages.

Unexpected attachments should also be approached cautiously. Phishing emails may contain documents, invoices, forms, or reports designed to install malware or capture information. Even if an attachment appears legitimate, users should verify its source before opening it. Unexpected files from unknown senders should generally be avoided.

Attackers frequently exploit current events to increase effectiveness. News stories, emergencies, natural disasters, financial developments, public health concerns, and major events often provide opportunities for fraudulent campaigns. Users should be especially cautious when receiving messages related to high-profile events because attackers often capitalize on public interest and concern.

Authentication codes have become valuable targets for cybercriminals. Many phishing attacks now attempt to obtain multifactor authentication codes in addition to passwords. Attackers may create convincing scenarios that persuade victims to share temporary verification codes. Legitimate organizations generally do not request authentication codes through unsolicited communications.

Artificial intelligence has introduced new challenges in the phishing landscape. Attackers can now generate highly convincing messages with proper grammar, personalized content, and realistic communication styles. AI tools may also assist in creating fake voices, images, and videos. As these technologies become more accessible, distinguishing legitimate communications from fraudulent ones may become increasingly difficult.

Fortunately, effective defenses exist. Verification remains one of the most powerful security practices. Instead of responding directly to suspicious messages, users should contact organizations through official channels. Calling a bank using the number printed on a card or visiting a company's official website provides greater confidence than relying on information contained within a message.

Developing a habit of slowing down significantly improves security. Most phishing attacks rely on impulsive reactions. Taking a moment to evaluate a situation, verify information, and consider alternatives often prevents mistakes. Patience can be one of the most effective cybersecurity tools available.

Education and awareness remain essential defenses. Attack techniques continue evolving, but the underlying principles often remain consistent. Attackers seek trust, urgency, emotion, and compliance. Users who understand these tactics become far more difficult targets. Knowledge transforms social engineering from a hidden threat into a recognizable pattern.

The most important lesson is that phishing attacks succeed because they target human behavior rather than technology. Security software can provide valuable assistance, but users remain the final line of defense. Awareness, skepticism, verification, and critical thinking significantly reduce the likelihood of becoming a victim.

By understanding how phishing, smishing, and social engineering attacks operate, smartphone users gain the ability to recognize warning signs, avoid manipulation, and protect sensitive information. In a world where communication channels continue expanding, these skills are becoming increasingly important for maintaining digital security.

Rebecca received a text message claiming that a package delivery

Rebecca considered herself cautious and responsible. She managed her finances carefully, stayed informed about current events, and used technology extensively for both personal and professional activities. Yet despite her confidence, she had never received formal cybersecurity training and assumed common sense would be enough to protect her from scams.

One busy morning, Rebecca received a text message claiming that a package delivery had failed due to an incomplete address. The message included a link and requested immediate verification. Since she had recently ordered several items online, the notification seemed reasonable. Without thinking much about it, she clicked the link.

The website looked professional and displayed familiar branding. It requested basic contact information and a small processing fee to complete delivery. Rebecca entered her details and submitted the payment. Within minutes, she received another notification from her bank regarding suspicious activity.

Alarmed, she contacted the bank directly and learned that the original message had been fraudulent. The website was a phishing page designed to collect personal and financial information. Although the bank quickly blocked unauthorized transactions, Rebecca felt embarrassed and frustrated. She had always considered herself too careful to fall for scams.

Determined to understand what happened, Rebecca began researching phishing attacks. She discovered that attackers specifically target ordinary individuals because they often trust familiar brands and routine communications. She learned how criminals use urgency, realistic designs, and emotional manipulation to influence behavior.

Several weeks later, Rebecca received another suspicious message. This time, the message claimed that her online banking account would be suspended unless she verified her identity immediately. Instead of reacting impulsively, she paused and carefully examined the details. The sender's number appeared unusual, and the message contained subtle grammatical inconsistencies.

Remembering what she had learned, Rebecca ignored the link and contacted her bank using the official phone number listed on her account. The representative confirmed that no issues existed and that the message was fraudulent. For the first time, Rebecca experienced the difference that awareness could make.

As her confidence grew, Rebecca became more attentive to suspicious communications. She noticed phishing attempts arriving through multiple channels. Some appeared as emails from online retailers. Others arrived through social media messages. A few came as automated phone calls claiming to represent government agencies. Once she understood the patterns, the warning signs became easier to recognize.

One afternoon, Rebecca's coworker Michael received a phone call from someone claiming to be a technical support representative. The caller stated that Michael's computer had been infected and requested remote access to fix the problem. Unsure how to respond, Michael asked Rebecca for advice.

She immediately recognized the scenario as a common social engineering tactic. Together, they contacted the actual technology provider, which confirmed that no such call had been initiated. Michael was relieved that he had sought a second opinion before taking action.

Over time, Rebecca became known among friends and family as someone knowledgeable about scams and cybersecurity. She taught relatives how to verify suspicious messages, identify phishing attempts, and recognize emotional manipulation. Many were surprised to learn how sophisticated modern attacks had become.

One evening, Rebecca's father received a call from someone claiming to represent a government agency. The caller threatened legal consequences unless immediate payment was made. Fearful and confused, he contacted Rebecca before responding. She explained that legitimate agencies do not typically demand immediate payment through unsolicited calls. Together, they verified that the call was fraudulent.

The incident reinforced an important lesson. Attackers often target emotions rather than technology. Fear, urgency, excitement, curiosity, and trust are powerful tools. Individuals who understand these tactics are far more likely to recognize scams before becoming victims.

As artificial intelligence technologies advanced, phishing attempts became even more convincing. Rebecca noticed improvements in grammar, personalization, and design quality. Some messages appeared nearly indistinguishable from legitimate communications. Yet despite these advancements, the underlying principles remained unchanged. Attackers still relied on manipulation, urgency, and deception.

Years after her first phishing experience, Rebecca reflected on how much her perspective had changed. What once seemed like an embarrassing mistake had become a valuable learning opportunity. She realized that cybersecurity is not about never making mistakes. It is about learning from experiences and continuously improving awareness.

Rebecca continued using technology confidently, but she approached communications differently. She verified unusual requests, examined links carefully, and avoided rushing important decisions. These habits required little effort yet provided substantial protection.

The experience taught her that cybersecurity is as much about psychology as technology. Understanding how people think, react, and make decisions is often more important than understanding software or hardware. Attackers exploit human behavior because it frequently provides the easiest path to success.

Most importantly, Rebecca learned that anyone can become a target. Intelligence, education, and experience do not guarantee immunity from deception. What matters is awareness, skepticism, and a willingness to verify information before taking action.

As she shared these lessons with others, Rebecca helped create a safer environment for her family, friends, and colleagues. Her story demonstrated that phishing attacks are not signs of personal failure. They are carefully designed manipulations created by individuals who understand human psychology.

By recognizing those tactics and responding thoughtfully, users can significantly reduce risk. The smartphone in Rebecca's pocket remained connected to the world, but it no longer served as an easy gateway for attackers. Awareness had transformed vulnerability into resilience.

In the years that followed, Rebecca encountered countless phishing attempts, scam messages, and social engineering schemes. Most were identified immediately because she understood the warning signs. The skills she developed became part of her daily life, protecting not only her information but also her confidence in navigating an increasingly connected digital world.

Her journey illustrated a simple but powerful truth: the strongest defense against social engineering is an informed and attentive mind. Technology can assist, but awareness remains the ultimate safeguard against deception.

Chapter 9

Safe Browsing, Secure Wi-Fi, and Protecting Your Mobile Internet Activity

Every day, billions of people use smartphones to access the internet for communication, shopping, banking, education, entertainment, work, and countless other activities. The internet provides extraordinary convenience and opportunities, but it also introduces risks that can affect privacy, security, finances, and personal information. Understanding how to browse safely, use wireless networks securely, and protect online activity is one of the most valuable skills modern smartphone users can develop. While many internet-based threats operate behind the scenes, informed users can significantly reduce risk through awareness and responsible habits.

When a smartphone connects to the internet, information constantly travels between the device and remote systems. Websites, applications, cloud services, search engines, streaming platforms, and online stores all exchange data with users. These interactions occur rapidly and often invisibly. Most users focus on the content they see on their screens without considering how information moves across networks or who may have access to it during transmission.

Understanding these processes helps users make safer decisions while online.

One of the most important concepts in internet security is encryption. Encryption transforms readable information into coded data that can only be understood by authorized parties. When websites use encryption properly, sensitive information such as passwords, payment details, messages, and personal data becomes significantly more difficult for attackers to intercept and read. Secure websites generally use HTTPS, which stands for Hypertext Transfer Protocol Secure. The presence of HTTPS indicates that communications between the browser and website are encrypted.

While HTTPS provides important protection, users should understand that it does not guarantee a website is trustworthy. Attackers can create fraudulent websites that also use encryption. A secure connection only means information is protected during transmission. Users must still evaluate whether a website itself is legitimate. Verifying domain names, checking for spelling inconsistencies, and avoiding suspicious links remain essential security practices.

Web browsers play a critical role in mobile security. Modern browsers include numerous protective features designed to identify malicious websites, block dangerous downloads, and warn users about suspicious activity. Keeping browsers updated ensures access to the latest security improvements. Users should also review browser privacy settings and understand how cookies, tracking technologies, and stored information affect online privacy.

Cookies are small files stored by websites to remember user preferences, login sessions, and browsing activity. While cookies often improve convenience, they can also contribute to extensive tracking. Advertising networks and analytics services frequently use cookies to build profiles of user behavior across multiple websites. Reviewing browser settings and periodically clearing stored data can help improve privacy.

Public Wi-Fi networks represent one of the most common internet-related security concerns. Airports, hotels, coffee shops, libraries, restaurants, shopping centers, and public venues frequently offer free internet access. While convenient, these networks may expose users to additional risks. Because public networks are shared by many individuals, attackers sometimes attempt to intercept communications, distribute malware, or create fraudulent access points.

One common attack involves rogue Wi-Fi networks. Cybercriminals create wireless networks with names that closely resemble legitimate services. For example, an attacker might create a network named "Airport_Free_WiFi" or "Hotel_Guest" to trick users into connecting. Once connected, users may unknowingly expose information to attackers who control the network. Verifying network names with staff or official sources helps reduce this risk.

Man-in-the-middle attacks represent another threat associated with insecure networks. In these attacks, criminals position themselves between users and legitimate services. Information transmitted through the network may be intercepted, modified, or monitored. While encryption reduces exposure, users should remain cautious when conducting sensitive activities on public networks.

Online banking, investment management, healthcare services, and business activities deserve particular attention when using public internet connections. Whenever possible, sensitive transactions should be conducted through trusted networks. Cellular data connections often provide stronger security than unknown public Wi-Fi networks because they rely on carrier-managed infrastructure and encryption mechanisms.

Virtual Private Networks, commonly known as VPNs, can provide additional protection during internet use. A VPN encrypts internet traffic and routes communications through secure servers. This process helps protect information from interception, particularly when using public networks. While VPNs do not eliminate all risks, they can significantly improve privacy and security when properly configured.

Search engines and websites collect substantial amounts of information about user behavior. Search queries, browsing histories, clicks, purchases, locations, and preferences often contribute to detailed profiles. Users concerned about privacy may wish to explore privacy-focused browsers, search engines, and settings that reduce data collection. Understanding how information is gathered allows individuals to make informed choices regarding online privacy.

Mobile advertisements also deserve attention. While most advertisements are legitimate, some may contain misleading claims, fraudulent offers, or links to malicious websites. Users should exercise caution when interacting with unfamiliar ads, particularly those promising unrealistic rewards, urgent warnings, or unexpected opportunities.

Downloads present another area of potential risk. Files obtained from websites may contain malware, spyware, ransomware, or other harmful software. Users should download content only from trusted sources and verify authenticity whenever possible. Unexpected downloads should be approached with caution, especially if they originate from unfamiliar websites or unsolicited communications.

Browser extensions and add-ons can enhance functionality but may also introduce security concerns. Some extensions request extensive permissions and collect significant amounts of data. Users should install extensions only from trusted developers and periodically review what has been added to their browsers.

Location privacy is increasingly important in the mobile environment. Websites and applications frequently request location access to provide services and recommendations. While location-based features can be useful, they may also reveal detailed information about habits, routines, and movements. Users should understand when location access is necessary and restrict permissions when appropriate.

Children and teenagers face unique online risks. Safe browsing practices should include education about scams, inappropriate content, online predators, misinformation, and privacy concerns. Parents and guardians can support safer internet use through communication, supervision, and appropriate technical controls.

Cybercriminals continuously adapt to changing technologies and user behavior. New websites, services, applications, and communication platforms create opportunities for innovation as well as new security challenges. Remaining informed about evolving threats helps users maintain effective protection over time.

Safe browsing ultimately involves a combination of technology, awareness, and judgment. Security tools provide valuable assistance, but users remain responsible for evaluating websites, protecting credentials, verifying information, and making informed decisions. Developing strong internet habits creates a foundation for safer online experiences across all devices and platforms.

The internet is one of humanity's most powerful resources, offering unprecedented access to information, communication, and opportunity. By understanding how to browse safely, use wireless networks responsibly, and protect online activity, smartphone users can enjoy these benefits while minimizing exposure to cyber threats. Knowledge and awareness remain essential companions in an increasingly connected world.

Olivia connected to a network labeled "Airport_Free_WiFi."

Olivia traveled frequently for work. Her smartphone served as her office, navigation system, banking center, communication hub, and entertainment device. Whether she was in airports, hotels, conference centers, or coffee shops, reliable internet access was essential to her daily routine. Because public Wi-Fi was widely available, she connected to wireless networks wherever she went without giving much thought to security.

One afternoon, while waiting for a flight at a busy airport, Olivia connected to a network labeled "Airport_Free_WiFi." The connection worked perfectly. She checked emails, reviewed business documents, accessed cloud storage, and completed several online tasks. The experience seemed completely normal.

Several days later, however, she began receiving unusual notifications. An email account reported suspicious login attempts. A social media platform requested password verification. A financial service notified her of access from an unfamiliar device. Although no immediate damage occurred, the pattern concerned her.

Olivia contacted her company's information security team for guidance. After reviewing the situation, the security specialist explained that the Wi-Fi network she had used might not have been legitimate. Attackers sometimes create fraudulent networks designed to attract travelers seeking free internet access. Once connected, users may unknowingly expose information or communications to monitoring.

The possibility was unsettling. Olivia had always assumed that if a network appeared official, it must be safe. The experience prompted her to learn more about internet security and wireless network risks. She quickly discovered that public Wi-Fi environments presented numerous opportunities for attackers.

Determined to improve her security practices, Olivia began making changes immediately. She verified network names before connecting, avoided conducting sensitive activities on unfamiliar networks, and installed a reputable VPN service. She also reviewed browser settings, strengthened passwords, and enabled multifactor authentication on critical accounts.

Several months later, Olivia encountered a situation that tested her new awareness. While staying at a hotel, she noticed multiple wireless networks with similar names. Instead of connecting automatically, she contacted the front desk to verify the correct network. The staff confirmed that one of the options was not associated with the hotel at all.

The incident reinforced the importance of caution. What previously seemed like a minor detail could have significant security implications. Olivia realized that attackers often rely on assumptions and convenience. Verifying information before acting disrupted many common attack strategies.

As her understanding grew, Olivia became increasingly interested in online privacy as well. She learned how websites track behavior, how advertising networks build user profiles, and how personal information moves across digital ecosystems. While she appreciated many benefits of personalized services, she also valued having greater control over her information.

One evening, while researching a product online, Olivia encountered a website offering an unbelievable discount. The offer seemed almost too good to be true. Remembering lessons about safe browsing, she examined the website more carefully. Several warning signs emerged, including unusual domain names, missing contact information, and inconsistent branding. Further investigation revealed numerous reports describing the site as fraudulent.

Years earlier, she likely would have proceeded without hesitation. Now, awareness helped her avoid potential financial loss. The experience demonstrated how cybersecurity knowledge influences everyday decision-making.

Olivia also began sharing what she learned with colleagues. During business trips, she encouraged coworkers to verify networks, use secure connections, and remain cautious about unfamiliar websites. Many admitted they had never considered the possibility of connecting to fake Wi-Fi networks or encountering malicious websites that appeared legitimate.

One coworker named Marcus later thanked her for the advice. While traveling overseas, he noticed several suspicious networks in an airport terminal. Because of Olivia's guidance, he avoided connecting and instead used his mobile carrier's data service. The decision may have prevented significant exposure.

As time passed, safe browsing became second nature for Olivia. She no longer viewed cybersecurity as a specialized technical field reserved for experts. Instead, she saw it as a practical life skill similar to locking doors, verifying identities, or reading contracts carefully. Small habits consistently applied provided meaningful protection.

Years after the airport incident, Olivia reflected on how much her perspective had evolved. The experience that initially seemed minor had transformed her approach to technology. She became more thoughtful, more informed, and more confident in navigating digital environments.

Importantly, she understood that internet security was not about avoiding technology. The internet remained an invaluable resource that enabled communication, productivity, education, and opportunity. The goal was not fear but informed use. Awareness allowed her to enjoy the benefits of connectivity while reducing unnecessary risks.

As wireless technologies continued advancing and new services emerged, Olivia remained committed to ongoing learning. She knew that cyber threats would continue evolving, but she also understood that the core principles of safe browsing remained remarkably consistent. Verify before trusting. Think before clicking. Protect sensitive information. Use secure connections. Remain aware of your surroundings.

These habits served her well throughout her personal and professional life. Whether working from a hotel, shopping online, communicating with clients, or exploring new destinations, she approached digital interactions with confidence and caution.

Looking back, Olivia considered herself fortunate to have learned these lessons before experiencing serious consequences. The internet offered tremendous opportunities, but it also required responsibility. By understanding how networks, websites, and online services operate, users gain the ability to make better decisions and protect themselves more effectively.

Her journey demonstrated that safe browsing is not a single action but a collection of habits practiced consistently over time. Those habits transformed potential vulnerabilities into strengths and allowed her to navigate an increasingly connected world with greater security and peace of mind.

The lesson remained clear: every internet connection represents both opportunity and responsibility. Users who understand this balance are better equipped to protect their information, preserve their privacy, and enjoy the benefits of the digital world safely and confidently.

Chapter 10

Building Your Personal Mobile Security Action Plan

Throughout this book, you have explored the foundations of mobile security. You have learned how smartphones store information, how cybercriminals target mobile users, how malware infections occur, how phishing attacks manipulate victims, how software updates protect devices, and how safe browsing habits reduce risk. While each topic is important individually, true security emerges when these concepts are combined into a consistent and practical strategy. Knowledge alone does not provide protection. Action transforms knowledge into security. The purpose of this chapter is to help you build a personal mobile security action plan that can guide your daily decisions and strengthen your defenses over the long term.

Many people approach cybersecurity reactively. They only think about security after a problem occurs. A stolen device, compromised account, financial loss, or privacy breach often becomes the event that finally motivates change. Unfortunately, reactive security usually means responding after damage has already occurred. A proactive approach is far more effective. Rather than waiting for an incident, users can take preventive measures that reduce the likelihood of becoming victims in the first place.

The first step in building a security action plan is understanding what you are protecting. Every individual has different priorities. Some users focus primarily on financial security. Others are concerned about privacy, family safety, professional responsibilities, personal communications, or intellectual property. Begin by identifying the information and services that matter most to you. Your banking applications, email accounts, photos, contacts, cloud storage, business documents, and social media accounts may all represent valuable assets. Knowing what you are protecting helps determine where security efforts should be concentrated.

Next, evaluate your current security posture honestly. Consider your passwords, authentication settings, application permissions, backup systems, update habits, browsing behavior, and privacy controls. Identify areas where improvements are needed. Many users discover weaknesses they were previously unaware of. The goal is not perfection but awareness. Security improvements begin with recognizing vulnerabilities before attackers do.

Strong authentication should serve as the foundation of any mobile security plan. Every important account should have a unique password or passkey. Multifactor authentication should be enabled whenever available, particularly for email accounts, financial services, cloud storage platforms, and social media accounts. Because email often serves as a recovery method for other services, protecting it deserves special attention.

Software maintenance should become a routine habit. Operating systems, applications, browsers, and security tools should remain current. Automatic updates provide an effective solution for many users. Consistent patching reduces exposure to vulnerabilities and ensures access to the latest security protections. Users who neglect updates gradually accumulate risk over time.

Application management is another critical component of a security action plan. Periodically review installed applications and remove those that are no longer needed. Evaluate permissions carefully and ensure that apps only have access to information necessary for their intended functions. Reducing unnecessary software and permissions minimizes opportunities for exploitation.

Backup strategies deserve careful consideration. Even the most secure devices can be lost, stolen, damaged, or affected by unexpected failures. A reliable backup system ensures that important information remains recoverable. Photos, documents, contacts, messages, and settings should be included in backup plans. Testing backups periodically provides confidence that recovery will be possible when needed.

Privacy management should also be incorporated into your action plan. Review account settings, advertising preferences, location permissions, and data-sharing practices. Understand what information applications collect and how that information is used. While complete privacy may be unrealistic in today's digital environment, informed choices allow users to maintain greater control over personal information.

Network security practices help protect internet activity. Users should exercise caution when connecting to public Wi-Fi networks and consider using VPN services when appropriate. Sensitive activities such as banking and financial transactions should generally be conducted through trusted networks. Verifying wireless networks before connecting helps reduce exposure to rogue access points.

Phishing awareness should remain an ongoing priority. Cybercriminals continually refine social engineering techniques. Developing habits such as verifying requests, examining links carefully, and avoiding impulsive reactions significantly improves protection. Remember that attackers often target emotions rather than technology. Awareness and patience are powerful defenses.

Device recovery planning is another important element. Ensure that location tracking services are enabled and understand how remote lock and remote wipe features operate. Record important account recovery information securely. If a device is lost or stolen, preparation allows faster and more effective responses.

Education should be viewed as a continuous process rather than a one-time activity. Cybersecurity threats evolve constantly. New technologies create new opportunities as well as new risks. Users who stay informed about emerging threats are better positioned to adapt. Following trusted cybersecurity resources, reading security news, and maintaining curiosity contribute to long-term resilience.

Family members often play important roles in personal security. A single compromised device within a household can affect multiple individuals. Discuss security practices with family members and encourage shared awareness. Children, teenagers, and older adults may require additional guidance regarding online risks, privacy concerns, and safe technology use.

Businesses frequently implement formal security programs because they understand the value of consistency. Personal cybersecurity benefits from a similar approach. Instead of relying on memory or good intentions, create a written action plan. Include specific tasks such as reviewing passwords, checking backups, updating software, auditing permissions, and evaluating privacy settings. Scheduled reviews help ensure that security remains a priority.

Risk management is a useful perspective when thinking about cybersecurity. The goal is not eliminating all risk because that is impossible. Instead, focus on reducing risk to acceptable levels. Every security measure contributes to a broader defense strategy. Strong passwords reduce credential theft risk. Updates reduce vulnerability risk. Backups reduce data loss risk. Awareness reduces social engineering risk. Together, these measures create meaningful protection.

It is also important to understand that cybersecurity is not about fear. News headlines often focus on dramatic attacks, massive breaches, and sophisticated threats. While these events are real, they do not mean individuals are powerless. On the contrary, many common threats can be mitigated through practical actions and responsible habits. Confidence comes from preparation, not from assuming risks do not exist.

Technology will continue changing rapidly. Artificial intelligence, connected devices, digital payments, cloud computing, biometric authentication, and emerging communication technologies will shape the future of mobile security. Some threats will disappear while new challenges emerge. However, the core principles of protection remain remarkably stable. Awareness, authentication, updates, backups, verification, privacy management, and responsible behavior continue providing strong foundations regardless of technological changes.

As you complete this book, remember that cybersecurity is a journey rather than a destination. There is no point at which security becomes complete or permanent. Instead, effective protection results from consistent effort, informed decision-making, and continuous learning. Every improvement strengthens your defenses and contributes to greater resilience.

Your personal mobile security action plan represents more than a checklist. It is a commitment to protecting your information, your identity, your finances, your relationships, and your future. By applying the lessons from this book consistently, you position yourself to enjoy the benefits of technology while reducing exposure to unnecessary risks.

The smartphone in your pocket connects you to opportunities, information, and people around the world. Protecting that connection is one of the most valuable investments you can make in your digital life.

A lost smartphone caused several stressful days

Anthony had always considered cybersecurity important, but like many people, he approached it inconsistently. He changed passwords occasionally, installed updates when convenient, and paid attention to obvious scams. Yet he lacked a clear strategy. Security decisions were often made reactively rather than proactively.

Over several years, Anthony experienced a series of minor incidents. A social media account was compromised after a password reuse issue. A phishing email nearly tricked him into revealing personal information. A lost smartphone caused several stressful days before it was recovered. None of these incidents caused catastrophic damage, but together they revealed a pattern. His security depended largely on luck rather than preparation.

One evening, Anthony decided to review every aspect of his digital life. He listed all major accounts, applications, devices, and online services he used regularly. The list was surprisingly long. Banking apps, investment platforms, email accounts, cloud storage services, healthcare portals, shopping websites, social media profiles, and dozens of mobile applications all contained valuable information.

The exercise helped him realize how interconnected everything had become. A compromise affecting one account could potentially affect many others. The realization motivated him to develop a more structured approach to security.

Anthony started by strengthening authentication. Weak passwords were replaced with unique credentials stored in a password manager. Multifactor authentication was enabled wherever possible. Recovery settings were reviewed carefully. The process required time, but the increased security provided peace of mind.

Next, he evaluated his smartphone itself. Unused applications were removed. Permissions were reviewed. Software updates were installed. Device tracking services were enabled. Backup systems were verified. Gradually, his smartphone transformed from a collection of loosely managed settings into a well-protected digital tool.

Several months later, Anthony encountered a situation that tested his preparations. While traveling, he accidentally left his smartphone in a rideshare vehicle. Realizing the mistake, he immediately accessed his account from another device, located the phone using tracking services, and contacted the driver. Because he had prepared in advance, recovery occurred quickly and securely.

The experience reinforced the value of planning. What could have become a stressful crisis became a manageable inconvenience. Preparation had created options.

As Anthony continued refining his security habits, he noticed something interesting. Cybersecurity no longer felt overwhelming. By breaking protection into manageable tasks and maintaining a structured plan, security became part of his routine. Small actions performed consistently produced significant results over time.

Friends often asked why he seemed so confident discussing cybersecurity topics. Anthony explained that confidence came from understanding and preparation rather than technical expertise. He was not a professional security analyst. He simply followed proven practices consistently.

One afternoon, a coworker named Sarah approached him for advice after receiving a suspicious message requesting account verification. Instead of responding immediately, she remembered Anthony's emphasis on verification. Together, they confirmed that the message was fraudulent. The incident demonstrated how awareness spreads when knowledge is shared.

Inspired by his own progress, Anthony began encouraging family members to create personal security plans as well. His parents strengthened passwords and enabled multifactor authentication. His younger brother improved backup practices and reviewed privacy settings. Small improvements across multiple individuals created stronger protection for everyone involved.

Years passed, and technology continued evolving. New devices, applications, and services entered Anthony's life. Yet the principles within his security plan remained relevant. Whenever new technologies appeared, he evaluated them using familiar questions. How is authentication handled? What information is collected? Are updates provided? How are backups managed? What risks exist?

These questions helped him navigate technological changes confidently. Instead of feeling overwhelmed by innovation, he applied consistent principles to new situations.

One evening, Anthony reviewed the security checklist he had created years earlier. Many items had become habits so deeply ingrained that he no longer thought about them consciously. Updates occurred automatically. Password management was routine. Verification became second nature. Privacy reviews happened periodically. Security was no longer an occasional concern; it was an integrated part of daily life.

Reflecting on his journey, Anthony realized that cybersecurity success rarely comes from dramatic actions. More often, it results from steady, deliberate choices made consistently over time. Strong defenses are built gradually through awareness, preparation, and discipline.

He also recognized that no plan could eliminate all risk. New threats would continue emerging. Mistakes would occasionally happen. Yet he felt prepared to respond because he had established strong foundations. Security was not about perfection; it was about resilience.

As Anthony looked toward the future, he remained optimistic. Technology would continue creating opportunities for learning, communication, business, and creativity. Cybersecurity challenges would undoubtedly evolve as well. However, the lessons he had learned provided confidence that he could adapt successfully.

The personal mobile security action plan he created years earlier had become much more than a document. It represented a mindset—one based on awareness, responsibility, and continuous improvement. That mindset protected not only his devices but also his identity, finances, relationships, and peace of mind.

Anthony often shared a simple message with others: cybersecurity begins with a decision to take ownership of your digital life. Tools and technologies are important, but they are most effective when combined with informed actions and consistent habits.

His story demonstrated that anyone can build strong security regardless of technical background. Success does not require advanced expertise. It requires commitment, awareness, and a willingness to act. By taking small steps consistently, individuals can create powerful defenses against modern cyber threats.

As the world became increasingly connected, Anthony remained confident because he understood a fundamental truth: security is not a destination. It is a journey of continuous learning, adaptation, and responsibility. By embracing that journey, he transformed cybersecurity from a source of concern into a source of empowerment.

The personal mobile security action plan he created years earlier had become much more than a document. It represented a mindset—one based on awareness, responsibility, and continuous improvement. That mindset protected not only his devices but also his identity, finances, relationships, and peace of mind.

Anthony often shared a simple message with others: mobile security begins with a decision to take ownership of your digital life. Tools and technologies are important, but they are most effective when combined with informed actions and consistent habits.

His story demonstrated that anyone can build strong security regardless of technical background. Security does not require advanced expertise—it requires commitment, awareness, and a willingness to act. By taking small steps consistently, individuals can create powerful defenses against modern cyber threats.

As the world became increasingly connected, Anthony remained confident because he understood a fundamental truth: security is not a destination. It is a journey of continuous learning, adaptation, and responsibility. By embracing that journey, he transformed a personal [illegible] concern into a source of empowerment.

Final Thoughts: Your Journey Toward a Safer Digital Future

As we reach the conclusion of *Mobile Security Fundamentals: How to Protect Your Smartphone, Personal Data, and Online Accounts From Modern Cyber Threats*, it is important to reflect on how much the role of the smartphone has evolved in our lives. What was once a simple communication device has become a gateway to our finances, relationships, careers, health information, personal memories, and daily activities. The smartphone is no longer just a piece of technology. It is a digital extension of who we are. Protecting it means protecting some of the most valuable aspects of our lives.

Throughout this book, you have explored the core principles of mobile security. You have learned about the modern threat landscape, how smartphones store and share information, the importance of strong security habits, authentication systems, physical device protection, software updates, malware prevention, phishing awareness, safe internet usage, and the development of a personal security action plan. Individually, each topic provides valuable protection. Together, they create a comprehensive foundation for safer and more confident technology use.

One of the most important lessons from this book is that cybersecurity is not reserved for experts. Many people assume that security is a highly technical field that requires advanced degrees, specialized certifications, or years of professional experience. While cybersecurity professionals certainly play important roles in protecting organizations and systems, individual users possess tremendous power to improve their own security. The simple choices made every day often determine whether attacks succeed or fail.

Strong passwords, multifactor authentication, regular software updates, cautious browsing habits, careful application management, and skepticism toward suspicious communications may seem ordinary. Yet these simple actions prevent countless security incidents every year. The reality is that many cybercriminals do not succeed because they possess extraordinary technical skills. They succeed because individuals fail to implement basic protections. By applying the lessons from this book, you dramatically reduce your vulnerability to many common threats.

Another key lesson is that cybersecurity is fundamentally about risk management. Perfect security does not exist. Every device, network, application, and system contains some level of risk. The goal is not to eliminate every possible threat. Instead, the goal is to reduce risk to manageable levels while continuing to enjoy the benefits of technology. Understanding this concept helps users approach security with confidence rather than fear.

Fear is often one of the biggest obstacles to cybersecurity education. News reports frequently highlight major data breaches, ransomware attacks, identity theft cases, and sophisticated cybercrime operations. While these threats are real, they can create the impression that individuals are powerless. In reality, informed users possess powerful tools for protecting themselves. Awareness, preparation, and responsible behavior remain among the most effective security measures available.

Knowledge alone, however, is not enough. Information becomes valuable only when translated into action. Reading about security practices is beneficial, but implementing those practices creates real protection. Consider the lessons from this book as a starting point rather than a finish line. Review your passwords. Enable multifactor authentication. Update your devices. Audit your applications. Verify your backups. Examine your privacy settings. Each action strengthens your defenses and contributes to long-term security.

Technology will continue evolving rapidly. Artificial intelligence, wearable devices, smart homes, connected vehicles, digital identities, virtual reality systems, and future innovations will create exciting opportunities. At the same time, new technologies inevitably introduce new risks. The specific threats may change, but the foundational principles of security remain remarkably consistent. Awareness, verification, authentication, updates, privacy management, and responsible behavior will continue providing protection regardless of how technology evolves.

Privacy deserves special attention as we move into an increasingly connected future. Every online interaction generates data. Smartphones, applications, websites, and services continuously collect information about behavior, preferences, movements, purchases, and communications. While some data collection supports useful services, users should remain aware of how information is gathered and shared. Privacy and security work together to create a safer digital environment.

You should also remember that cybersecurity extends beyond personal protection. Your actions can affect family members, friends, coworkers, and organizations. A compromised account may expose contacts to phishing attacks. An infected device may spread malware. Weak security practices can create broader risks. Conversely, strong habits help create safer digital communities. By protecting yourself, you contribute to the security of others as well.

Families play a particularly important role in cybersecurity. Children and teenagers are growing up in a world where mobile devices are present from an early age. Teaching safe habits, critical thinking, privacy awareness, and responsible online behavior can provide lifelong benefits. Older adults may also benefit from guidance regarding scams, phishing attacks, and fraud prevention. Security awareness should be viewed as an ongoing conversation rather than a one-time lesson.

One of the most encouraging aspects of cybersecurity is that improvement is always possible. You do not need to become perfect overnight. Small improvements accumulate over time. Replacing a weak password today, enabling multifactor authentication tomorrow, reviewing app permissions next week, and updating devices regularly can collectively create substantial protection. Progress matters more than perfection.

Cybercriminals thrive when users are unaware, distracted, rushed, or complacent. The habits developed throughout this book help counter those vulnerabilities. Taking a moment to verify information, thinking critically about requests, maintaining updated software, and protecting account access all make you a far more difficult target. Attackers generally prefer easy opportunities. Strong security habits encourage them to move elsewhere.

It is also important to maintain balance. Cybersecurity should support your use of technology rather than interfere with it. The goal is not to avoid innovation or disconnect from the digital world. Instead, the goal is to use technology confidently and responsibly. Security measures should empower users, not limit them. When implemented effectively, security becomes a natural part of everyday life rather than a constant source of concern.

As you continue your journey, remain curious. Cybersecurity is one of the fastest-changing fields in the world. New threats, tools, technologies, and best practices emerge constantly. Individuals who continue learning remain better prepared to adapt. Curiosity and education are powerful defenses against evolving risks.

The smartphone in your pocket provides access to opportunities previous generations could scarcely imagine. You can communicate instantly across continents, manage businesses remotely, access vast libraries of information, conduct financial transactions, learn new skills, and connect with communities worldwide. These capabilities are extraordinary. Protecting them is worth the effort.

The future will undoubtedly bring new cybersecurity challenges. However, it will also bring new defensive technologies, stronger protections, and greater awareness. The individuals who thrive in this environment will not necessarily be the most technical. They will be the most informed, adaptable, and responsible users.

As you finish this book, remember that cybersecurity is not a destination. It is an ongoing commitment to protecting what matters most. Every secure choice strengthens your defenses. Every lesson learned increases your resilience. Every habit developed contributes to a safer digital life.

Thank you for investing your time in learning the fundamentals of mobile security. The knowledge you have gained can help protect your information, preserve your privacy, secure your finances, safeguard your relationships, and strengthen your confidence in an increasingly connected world.

The threats are real, but so are the solutions.

The future of your digital security begins with the choices you make today.

Thank you for investing your time in learning the fundamentals of mobile security. The knowledge you have gained can help protect your information, preserve your privacy, secure your finances, safeguard your relationships, and strengthen your confidence in an increasingly connected world.

www.ingramcontent.com/pod-product-compliance
Lightning Source LLC
LaVergne TN
LVHW040520210926
848480LV00007BA/1526